D1193855

YANKEE YARNS

YANKEE YARNS

BY

Alton H. Blackington

DODD, MEAD & COMPANY
NEW YORK, 1954

Published September, 1954
Second Printing, November, 1954

Library of Congress Catalog Card Number: 54-11233

Printed in the United States of America
by The Cornwall Press, Inc., Cornwall, N. Y.

This book is dedicated to

Charles F. Haywood

whose sagacity and zeal I have much admired,
leaned upon and sometimes,
I fear, abused.

This book is dedicated to

Charles F. Haywood

Whose sagacity and zeal I have much admired,
leaned upon and sometimes,
I fear, abused.

Acknowledgments

To all the interested listeners who sent us tips, clippings and photographs on these and other *Yankee Yarns*, and to the many kind-hearted persons who went out of their way to show us around the scene of action, to others who loaned us books and valuable documents, I shall be eternally grateful. Considering that I have been gathering these stories over a period of many years, the names of the people who have helped me run into the hundreds.

In addition to those mentioned in the text who have been of assistance, I wish especially to thank the following:

J. Sanger Attwill, Miss Carrie Bangs and others of North Lubec, Maine, Laurence B. Brown, the late Judge Nelson P. Brown, George Calvin Carter, Robert B. Choate (Boston HERALD), the late Sam E. Conner (Lewiston JOURNAL), Charles H. P. Copeland (Peabody Museum, Salem), Judge Arthur Comley, Edward L. Davis (personal secretary to Thomas W. Lawson), Ernest S. Dodge (Peabody Museum), J. Marshall Duane (First National Stores, Inc.), Oscar H. Dunbar.

Wendell S. Hadlock (William A. Farnsworth Library and Art Museum, Rockland), Waldo F. Glover, Harland Little, Henry McWay, A. G. Owen, Philip D. Phair (Presque Isle, Maine), John M. Richardson (Rockland COURIER-GAZETTE), Robb Sagendorph (YANKEE magazine), Harold E. Severance (Severance Lodge, Center Lovell, Maine), Col. George L. Smith (Peabody Museum), Albert Snow.

Edward Rowe Snow, W. Gordon Swan (WBZ-TV), John I. Taylor (Boston GLOBE), Donald G. Trayser, George E. Tufts, Ernie Tucker (Beverly TIMES), Miss Dorothy Vaughan (Portsmouth, N. H. library), Carl T. Warton, the late Frank A. Winslow.

Finally, there would have been no *Yankee Yarns* without the assistance given me by a great number of libraries, historical societies, museums and newspapers. How can I possibly thank them enough for all they have done for me?

Foreword

EVER SINCE I WAS a high school student in Rockland, Maine, whenever I have met an interesting character or a worth while person in any field of endeavor, I have asked questions, listened attentively and made notes. If I read a human interest story or historical document, I clipped or noted it. In this way I was copying Frank A. Winslow of the Rockland COURIER-GAZETTE whose footsteps I dogged as a boy. He was my idol.

When I enlisted in the Navy during World War I and my family moved from Maine to Massachusetts, we brought a minimum of household goods, but what seemed a ton of books, papers, pictures, relics and souvenirs—all of them tips to good stories.

Joining the staff of the Boston HERALD after the war, I had exceptional opportunities to travel with note book and camera and meet interesting people, from old ladies who lived in haunted houses with forty cats to President Calvin Coolidge. I covered fires, floods, shipwrecks and celebrities, always watching for the unusual, human interest angle. I poked through country cemeteries and visited local libraries and historical societies.

It was natural, with all this material and thousands of negatives, that I drifted into lecturing, which in my case was story telling. After each show, someone always came up to ask, "Have you put these *Yarns* into book form?" And I always answered, "Not yet. Someday."

In 1933 I got into radio, and from then until 1953, *Yankee Yarns* was broadcast practically every week over WBZ, Boston, and the New England stations of NBC. We received thousands of requests, but it was impossible to send out copies of the scripts folks wanted. So we promised someday to write a book. Many listeners thought all I had to do was hand a publisher a batch of radio scripts and the book would be born. It's not that easy. Writing for listening is one thing, for reading something else. I have been told that I am a better story teller than writer. I know little about the finer points of literary composition and am a naturally poor speller. I have my own system of punctuation and the radio scripts were generally undecipherable to anyone but me.

It is only fair that proper credit be given to the one who has waded through this morass of manuscript and helped me produce the MS. from which these pages are printed. I refer, of course, to my wife, Alice Powers Blackington, who besides doing this, has driven our car thousands of miles so we could get these *Yarns*, made millions of stenographic pothooks, answered radio and TV mail, and somehow managed to cook and keep house as I think only a daughter of Maine can.

We both realize that in spite of our efforts there may be mistakes, but at last the job is done, and here is the first volume of *Yankee Yarns* for all the people who over the years have wanted to read them, and for Yankees everywhere.

A. H. B.

May 28, 1954
Beverly Farms, Massachusetts

Contents

The Luck of the Lawsons 1
"Dug-out" Dan 31
Thunderbolt 45
Mrs. Hiller's Funeral 61
Circus Queen 70
The Petrified Indian Boy 88
Gold Mine Hoax 96
Sea Water Gold 105
Palestine Pilgrimage 119
Human Hibernation 134
The Dugway 150
Molasses Disaster 164
Runaway Pond 172
Presque Isle Lynching 182
Ruth Blay 193
The Legend of Micah Rood 202
Runaway Locomotives 212
Steamer *Portland* 219

The Luck of the Lawsons

PART ONE

I SHALL ALWAYS BE THANKFUL I was born on the Maine coast where every member of the family and most of our neighbors took an active and personal interest in the weather, and paid strict attention to folklore, signs, omens and various old-time superstitions.

From the moment I crept out of bed to patter barefoot downstairs to breakfast, till Father banked the fire at night and Mother put the cats out and peeked for stars, we were weather conscious. We had no daily newspaper nor radio reports, but all the folks who lived on the West Meadow Road, some two miles inland from the city of Rockland, Maine, subscribed to the *Old Farmer's Almanac*, and in our house it dangled from a dingy string fastened to the edge of the lamp shelf back of the kitchen stove. Long before I was old enough to digest all the fine print in the

Almanac's tightly-packed pages, I had been taught the meaning of the mystical signs of the zodiac, and my folks had told me which of the common weather signs could be relied upon.

"Red in the morning, sailor take warning.
Red at night, sailor's delight"

was surely dependable, as was

"Mackerel-back sky and old mares' tails,
make tall ships carry low sails."

But not always did "rain before seven" mean that it would "clear before eleven."

Besides these weather signs, which were seemingly countless, there were other bucolic omens having to do with the planting of crops, harvesting, the slaughtering of hogs, and so on. It was bound to be messy business if you made sauerkraut so that it would ripen and "work" at the full of the moon. "If the moon can raise the Atlantic ocean," they said, "it sure can lift the juice out of a sauerkraut keg."

The farmers always thought it brought good luck to nail up a horseshoe, and none in our neighborhood would ever pull a nail from a horse's hoof without driving it immediately into a pine post—otherwise the injured animal would contract blood poisoning and have to be shot.

Wild birds flying into the house were regarded as a warning of death, as was the continued howling of a hound dog in the night. I can recall how scared we children used to be when we went to visit up-country cousins and slept in their old-fashioned feather bed, where invariably we heard the eerie ticking of the so-called "death watch" in the massive headboard. Entomologists know that this noise is caused by a tiny beetle–Anobium tessellatum–standing on his hind legs and banging his head to attract his mate. But to us, this meant that someone was sure to die.

Along our shores there were superstitions about the sea and ships which haunted every port. Playing around the wharves and shipyards of Rockland, Maine, I heard a lot of them. We all knew that it was bad luck to whistle on shipboard. This probably came from the fact that if a dozen lusty sailors whistled at the same time, the bo'sun's mate's whistle could not be heard, but some believed that whistling brought on wind.

Most old-time skippers never liked to have a minister or woman come aboard, but children, aside from being a nuisance, were considered lucky. Rats, cats and cockroaches were expected to be on vessels, but a black cat was tabu. And if a cat, roach or rat was seen leaving a ship just before she sailed, superstitious sailors walked off too, rather than take a chance on a ship which was doomed.

If a workman was killed while the ship was building, she was said to be "launched in blood" and therefore jinxed. If she caught fire, or stuck on the ways, or was sent to sea without being properly christened, she was most certainly hoodooed, and once thus cursed, nothing could clear her of suspicion.

One of the most famous "hoodooed" ships was the world's largest schooner, *Thomas W. Lawson*, launched from the Bethlehem yard at Fore River, Quincy, on July 10, 1902.

Millions of words have been written about the man for whom this schooner was named—a Boston boy who rose from rags to riches to become a fire-ball of finance, defying the sharpest brains of State and Wall Streets. He was "the arch-enemy of Standard Oil," "the king of Amalgamated Copper," a man who thought nothing of making or losing a million dollars over night. He was born on February 26, 1857, in Charlestown, Massachusetts, on one of the streets leading to the Bunker Hill Monument. His father, a "poor but respectable" carpenter, as the Alger books of that time would have said, had migrated from Nova Scotia to Boston in search of work. While Tom was still a toddler, the family moved to Cambridgeport, taking a tenement not too far from Central Square, and there Tom grew up and went to school.

Unlike the kids who plan to be policemen, or drive the fire engine, Tom always wanted to be a banker. Acting on a boyish hunch one winter day in 1869, he left his humble home determined to find a niche in the banking business. Running across Longfellow bridge, he was soon in Boston's bustling Bowdoin Square. Then, threading through the streets to Washington, he turned into State, admiring the imposing office buildings and the well dressed gentlemen wearing tall silk hats who worked there.

In the window of Amory, Stevens & Co., Brokers, he saw a sign: OFFICE BOY WANTED. Stamping the snow from his rubbers, he leaned against the heavy door and barged in.

A clerk, peering down at the flushed boyish face, barely

level with the counter, asked, "What can I do for you, young man?"

Tom pointed to the sign, saying eagerly, "I want that job!"

Everyone who heard his high-pitched voice stopped, stared, then snickered. The clerk explained tartly, "What we want is an older, bigger boy."

Eleven-year-old Tom didn't budge. Instead, in well chosen words, he gave such a sales talk about his qualifications, darned if they didn't decide to give him a try. He peeled off his jacket and went to work.

But that night his mother boxed his ears, for skipping school, and next day dragged him back to the class room. Tom, having a hunch he belonged at 39 State Street, skipped away at recess time and dashed back to Amory, Stevens & Co. A conference was held between Mr. Amory and Tom's mother, and it was agreed that if he would study nights and week ends, he could continue working. Two weeks later, on his twelfth birthday, Tom told his Cambridge pals, "State Street is the place for me; I like being a broker!"

For Christmas that year his boss gave him a bonus—a fresh, crisp hundred dollar bill (more than his hard working father earned in ten weeks). Instead of saving it, Tom scoured the best stores in Boston, buying costly gifts for his mother and sisters. Even then, he liked "the best."

During the next two years he was kept busy weighing out gold in the Company's scales, keeping accounts and running errands for the heads of departments. This brought him in contact with the biggest bankers of the day, and by observing, he soon learned that fortunes could be made by the ups and downs of the stock market. He was just fourteen when he took his first flyer.

Because his judgment was sound, he made a few hundred, and, thus encouraged, he kept on investing, but only when the "signs" were favorable, or he had a strong hunch. It suddenly dawned on Amory, Stevens that in young Tom Lawson, they had an exceptional office boy. About this time he was given an important assignment which he handled with the finesse of a veteran.

Amory, Stevens were financial agents for the Cincinnati, Sandusky and Cleveland Railroad, of which Rush R. Sloan, a big-shot in banking and Member of Congress, was president. It came as a great shock, then, when word was flashed that President Sloan had grabbed the railroad's books and securities and fled on his yacht to Canada, just out of reach of American authorities. A vast amount of money was involved, and unless things could be patched up quickly, Amory, Stevens stood to lose millions.

Negotiations for return of the securities were opened between the road's owners and Sloan; as the most active negotiator, Amory, Stevens dispatched a messenger from Boston. That messenger was Thomas Lawson. Hiring a small steamboat, he sailed across Lake Erie to the Canadian side and tied up to Mr. Sloan's yacht. Papers were exchanged, consummating a compromise, and Tom hastened back to Boston.

The market value of Sandusky stock before this trouble had been $56. Then it dropped to $3 per share. Back in

Boston, Tom rounded up his pals and formed a pool, buying the stock until it went to $22 a share. Then, acting on a hunch, Tom advised, "Time to sell," which they did, making a handsome profit. Lawson's share of the deal was about $50,000!

On his seventeenth birthday, Thomas Lawson had $60,000 in the bank from this and other operations on the Street.

He dabbled in Boston water-power stock, which at that time was rising and falling like the tide at T wharf, and he decided money was to be made by selling short. Not having the inside dope he had on the Sandusky deal, he was on the wrong side of the market this time, and awoke one morning to find that the Boston aldermen had passed a land bill which made the stock go up sharply. He was short, clear up to his neck; the stock was rising fast, and he had to cover. $59,840 of his savings was gone with the wind!

To make a clean sweep, Lawson spent the remainder of his savings on a dinner for his friends at Young's Hotel. When the check was paid, he had just $4.30 left in his pocket. In a "grand gesture" which marked him forever, he called the head waiter and said. "Here, this is for you." And walked out onto the street flat broke.

At seventeen, Lawson had made and lost what most men would have considered a fortune.

It took him two years to get back on his feet financially, this time by promoting a new type of printing machine for turning out theatre tickets in rolls. By the time he was twenty-one, he had purchased a pair of fine black horses, got married, and had roughly $900,000 to his credit.

The Lawsons lived in Cohasset, and frequently took long rides along the South Shore, usually to Egypt and Scituate. One day when they stopped to let the horses graze on a hill overlooking the Otis farm and the ledges and ocean beyond, Mrs. Lawson said wistfully, "I wish we could build a house on top of this hill, and have a nice white fence and some rambler roses."

Lawson was tough to his business rivals, but he was more than generous to those he loved. Before the sun set that night he had purchased the Otis place and lots of land besides, and by the next day he was laying his plans before a group of builders and landscape gardeners.

"One year from today," he said, fingering his favorite jade elephant, "I want this house ready to move into. Ledges? Blast them out! Poor soil? Get some that's good! Now get to work!"

The new home was called "Dreamwold." The house, a gray shingled, two-story affair of twenty-two rooms, surrounded by imported shrubs, flowers and trees, was unlike anything around Boston.

At either side of the main entrance was a sizable guest house, and nearby were smaller cottages for the help, a dove cote, kennels for Lawson's blooded dogs, and a picturesque windmill. The stable which housed his thoroughbred horses was eight hundred feet long with a riding hall nearby. (Later, after Lawson's luck deserted him, this stable was moved to the Brockton Fair grounds and became the Agricultural Building.)

Around the entire estate of three hundred and fifty acres, Lawson had built a beautiful fence, painted white and covered with his wife's favorite variety of rambler rose. Hearing her tell a nursery man that she liked a special kind of carnation, Lawson spent $30,000 to propagate it, and almost always wore one of the carnations in his buttonhole.

Because Mrs. Lawson loved organ music, Tom ordered a pipe organ for "Dreamwold" which cost $100,000, and then, finding that it had to be power-operated, he built an elaborate water-power plant just to pump the immense bellows.

He engaged famous artists to hand decorate the dining room, with a frieze of golden grain fields, ripening grapes, orchards ablaze with red ripe fruit and other festive farm scenes. Over the massive table he hung a huge, pumpkin-shaped stained glass globe, made by Tiffany at a cost of several thousand dollars. At his famous dinners, the golden globe cast rays of yellow light upon spotless linen and shining silver. Around the edge of the fireplace, especially fired tiles carried out the pumpkin motif, while in back was an elaborate secret vault—which held goodness knows what interesting things in those extravagant times.

All the sleeping rooms were decorated with Japanese silk and satin brought from the Orient. Each room had its own fireplace and bath, rare luxuries to even the wealthiest. Mrs. Lawson's own boudoir in this lavish home was a marvel of glass, mirrors and solid gold and silver, and her private tub was hewn from a single block of imported marble by the best Italian craftsmen. When Mrs. Lawson died in

1906, her room was closed, but every day for eighteen years it was cleaned and dusted with meticulous care by servants who were ordered by the heart-broken husband not to move even comb or hairpin as much as an inch.

Thomas Lawson was one of the most superstitious men who ever lived. His life was ruled by hunches, dreams, signs, symbols and numbers. If he lost, he blamed his ill fortune onto "unfriendly signs" and the number thirteen. If he won, he attributed his good luck to the number three. He located his Boston office at 33 State Street, and had as his private telephone number: 333. His business associates often commented on the way he bought stock—never in blocks of one hundred or a thousand, but instead, lots of three hundred thirty-three shares, or multiples of three.

Those who knew him intimately said he was always nervous and irritable on Fridays, and whenever that day of the week fell on a thirteenth, he went into a blue funk. It was fate, he said, that the great schooner *Thomas W. Lawson* was wrecked on a Friday the thirteenth. "There are thirteen letters in her name and mine," he explained, "and also in the name of the Sun Oil Company to which she was leased."

To counteract—somewhat—the evil signs around him, Lawson collected elephants, which he believed were lucky. He owned hundreds of them: wood, glass, china, ebony, jade, gold. They guarded his office desk; they were everywhere in his home in Winchester; they marched in parades along the mantels at "Dreamwold."

At the height of his spectacular career Thomas W. Lawson was estimated to be worth $35,000,000, including jewels, art treasures, books, and all the wonderful furnishings of his dream home at Egypt, Massachusetts. When luck turned against him and he lost his money and health, everything went under the auctioneer's hammer, scattered to the four winds, so that even his children did not know where these objects went.

However, one of his most remarkable possessions years later came to light in the hands of a Boston jeweler. This is the wonderful watch made by Tiffany of New York at a cost of $10,000. Tom Lawson considered it his most powerful talisman of all, and in the light of what happened on several occasions, we can hardly quarrel with his superstitious belief, or blame him for his faith in the virtues of this treasure.

I am indebted to Carl Warton, feature writer for the Boston Sunday *Herald*, for this story. Mr. Warton permitted me to use it on the radio, on television, and agreed with me that it should be included in this collection of *Yankee Yarns*.

It was a cool spring day in 1899 when Mr. Lawson, faultlessly dressed as became his station in the financial world, and wearing one of his wife's favorite carnations, stepped into Tiffany's in New York and asked to see the manager.

"I want you to build me a watch," he said earnestly, "that will have a number of things, chimes and so forth. You will find the specifications on this paper. Look it over, please, and then write me when the watch will be ready and what it will cost. Thank you, and good day."

A month or so later, Lawson received a reply from the manager of Tiffany's. In brief, he said, "While you have asked us to do almost the impossible, we can have a watch made to your directions in Switzerland. But it will take the most expert Swiss craftsman at least a year of painstaking work and it will cost roughly about $10,000."

That was all right with Lawson, and he signed the order.

It was over a year before the new watch was delivered, and as he took it from its case, Tom Lawson felt a warm glow of satisfaction. Some inner psychic feeling comforted him as he held it in his hand, gazing at the familiar faces of his family wondrously engraved on the outside of the heavy gold case. One cover bore a likeness of himself and three of his children, while on the other was a delicately etched portrait of his wife and the other three children.

In the stem of the watch was a beautiful alexandrite, a semi-precious stone from Russia which glows green in daylight and red at night. (Lawson also had an alexandrite ring, alexandrites being so lucky.)

It was in the works of this timepiece, however, that the magic of expert watchmaking was demonstrated. A whole set of chimes had been reduced to vest-pocket size and installed to work at the whim of Thomas Lawson. For instance, each week-day morning at nine forty-five, a gong would tinkle, telling the broker that in a quarter hour the stock market would open. Those fifteen minutes were often important to him, as any stock broker will understand. At ten o'clock, when actual trading began, the gong sounded again, not a raucous ring like an alarm clock, but a musical note, signifying business was at hand. And it sounded again at two forty-five, reminding the wizard of State Street that but a quarter of an hour remained of that trading day. The final bell rang at three when the market closed.

On Saturdays, without any attention from its owner, that wonderful watch would ring just before the ten o'clock opening of the market and again at twelve o'clock closing, instead of three.

That is not all of those magic chimes. While Lawson was entertaining dinner guests he frequently forgot the time, so promptly at seven forty-five another bell tinkled to remind him it was time to exercise his dogs. By the time it rang again at eight, he was on his way to the kennels.

There were other features to this timepiece, too. Besides telling the time, in minutes, hours and seconds, extra hands indicated the day of the week, the month and year.

Tom Lawson carried the watch every day, firmly believing that it brought him good luck, and when he retired at night, he placed it on a bedside table within easy reach. If, in the darkness, he awakened and wanted to know the time, he simply pulled a tiny clip on the side of the watch, and, pronto, a low pitched gong would sound off the hours, then the minutes in blocks of five. If, for example, the hour was three-thirty A.M., one chime would sound three times, followed by another which would ring six times. Thus he could always know the time, within five minutes, at any period of the night.

While this timepiece cost Lawson thousands of dollars, it was not its wizardry of watch-making, nor its intrinsic value that caused him to prize it so highly. For him, it meant prosperity, personal safety. He intended to have it always with him; when he did forget it, he invariably had bad luck.

At one time, Lawson had one hundred horses at "Dreamwold." Some were bred to race, others were saddle and show horses. He had a splendid private race track, and day after day, in the early morning, he would climb to the judges' tower overlooking the track and clock his racers. One of them, "Boralma," showed such speed and fortitude, Lawson decided to enter him in the Kentucky Derby. After several weeks of careful clocking by his wonderful watch, Lawson was positive that "Boralma" had what it takes. Accustomed to doing things in a grandiose manner, he had a box car prepared, then hired a special train to take horse, family, friends and members of the press to Louisville. This was given much space in the newspapers, and many of the Boston party, acting on Lawson's assurance, placed heavy bets on "Boralma."

The special train from Massachusetts arrived in a flurry of high hopes. "Boralma" was transferred to his stable. Trainers and stablemen were at a great pitch of excitement. The party was feverishly keyed up. But the usually affable Lawson was missing—he had suddenly discovered that his lucky watch was back in "Dreamwold," on his dresser; he slipped out and took the next train home. The note he left said, "I don't want to be there when 'Boralma' loses!"

"Boralma" did lose, and so did all who had bet on him.

Without any doubt the strangest story of all which attaches to the wondrous watch is the part played in connection with the ill-fated schooner *Thomas W. Lawson.* This was the first all-steel sailing ship to be built at the Bethlehem yard in Quincy, and as plans progressed for the ship's construction, many a hot argument arose over the number of masts she should have. Designer Crowninshield suggested seven, and this was agreeable to the owners, but because there had never been a seven-masted schooner, many veteran skippers frowned on the idea, pointing out that in rough weather and high winds she would be wholly unmanageable.

Captain John G. Crowley, her builder, had already launched the first six master (*Geo. W. Wells*) at Camden, Maine, and he argued that with a sturdy hull of steel, the new ship could easily carry an extra mast; this opinion was shared by his brother, Arthur Crowley, who was to be her captain. John Wardwell, veteran designer and builder of ships in Rockland, Maine, disagreed.

Because Tom Lawson was the biggest share holder and the ship was to bear his name, he was naturally interested, and for many nights, after a hard day at his State Street office, he pondered the question. Should they use six masts, or seven?

There came a day when the decision had to be made, and the night before, Tom Lawson retired early and fell into a deep sleep. Buried in his subconscious mind, however, was the problem of the masts. Six or seven? Six or seven? Sometime before dawn, he awoke with a start as if someone had touched him. He listened intently, but heard only the dripping of the fog-drenched trees and the chirping of a cricket under his window.

Why, he asked himself, did I wake up like this? And as he listened in the darkness, he heard the faithful tick of his watch. Putting out his hand he touched the tiny lever and instantly heard the chimes: one, two, three, four, five, six.

That's it! he said to himself. There's my answer. The *Thomas W. Lawson* will have six masts. I'll tell them in the morning. And with that load off his mind, he went back to sleep.

But when he reached his office and put in a call to the shipyard, he disregarded the still small voice he had heard in the night. He could not resist the temptation to outdo his competitors. The idea of building the world's largest sailing vessel had always appealed to him. He had done things in a big way before; he would again.

And so, he said, "I've decided she better be a seven master."

With Lawson's vote, the plan for seven masts was carried out, and work went ahead. Had he taken the warning which his good luck watch gave, and stuck to six masts, the great schooner might have worked her way out of her dangerous situation between rocks and shore off Land's End, England, but, not being able to wear around with her seven masts in time, she was caught, smashed on the ledges, and went down, on Friday the thirteenth, December, 1907!

Ten years later, another incident occurred which illustrates the faith Tom Lawson had in his watch, and how helpless he became without it. Lawson had made a statement to the press that, having obtained advance knowledge of what President Woodrow Wilson was going to say to Congress, he had cleaned up in the market. Summoned to appear before an investigating committee to explain the leak, Lawson bumped into Secretary Tumulty, also on his way to the committee room.

Tumulty, glancing at his watch, saw that it had stopped. He called, "What time is it, Mr. Lawson?" And Lawson, reaching in his pocket, found to his horror that he had forgotten his lucky timepiece; then he recollected having left it on the mantel of the living room at "Dreamwold." He was so distracted, friends thought he had suffered a stroke, but he went before the committee nevertheless. The outcome of that hearing, as is well known, dealt a body blow to the Lawson interests. Shaky, perspiring and faltering in his answers, the financier went to pieces and made an extremely poor impression.

From that day, Lawson's power declined. Wall Street ceased to fear him. Carl Warton's article in the Boston Sunday *Herald* concludes, "It is generally accepted that the collapse of the Lawson fortune started that day in 1917 when Thomas W. Lawson appeared before Government investigators without his lucky watch!"

I saw this fabulous watch a few years ago, in the office of Edmund Luftig, a Boston jeweler, and inspected it closely. The alexandrite stone had been removed from the stem, and replaced by a garnet. The case was beautiful; I noticed that around the face of Tom Lawson, an angel spread protecting wings; there were many symbolic streamers and figures. There were six separate hands, all in good working order, but some of the special chimes, after half a century, no longer performed as they did for the wizard of State Street.

Mr. Luftig admitted that the timepiece was for sale, but

I could not get him to set a price. I wondered if he was superstitious about it. He well might have been, considering that his address was 333 Washington Street!

PART TWO

Any time you want to start an argument, just bring up the subject of the world's only seven-masted schooner and see what happens. No one can deny that she was the largest schooner ever built, and few will deny that she proved to be jinxed, but on the question of names for her masts few will agree. Before the days of such big sailing ships, masts were called fore, main, mizzen. Then came the spanker and jigger, and when Captain John G. Crowley launched his first six-master (*George W. Wells*) from the Bean Yard in Camden, Maine, he designated the sixth mast as driver, and he jokingly suggested that the seventh mast on the *Lawson* be known as the pusher. Landlubber reporters were familiar with the "fore, main, mizzen" combination, but invariably got all balled up with the "spanker, jigger, driver, pusher" idea. A clipping from the Boston *Globe* states that as many as thirty different combinations of those names have been used in connection with the *Lawson.*

While this controversy was at its height, I dropped in on Captain Charles Magee of Rockland, Maine, and asked his opinion.

"All I know," he said, "is what I was told when I went on the *Lawson* as mate. There had been such a mixup that Designer Crowninshield, Builder Crowley and Masterrigger Harold Hansen got together and issued an official list. It ran, as I recall, like this: fore, main, mizzen, middle, jigger, spanker and pusher. But with constantly changing crews, most of the men simply referred to the masts by number—one to seven."

I inquired if he ever heard the Lawson's masts called Monday, Tuesday, Wednesday and so forth, after the days of the week. Captain Magee snorted. "Not while I was mate! That's all newspaper guff! Like the stories you read about the *Lawson* being hard to handle. Why, with eight thousand tons of coal in her hold and in a good breeze, she was the sweetest thing I ever sailed on, and fast, too. We used to pass steam freighters like they were standing still!"

I mentioned Tom Lawson's pet superstitions and the popular belief that the schooner was hoodooed, but Captain Magee shrugged and snorted again. "All this business about the *Lawson* being jinxed," he said, "started when it was announced that her keel was to be laid on November first, 1901. That was a Friday, and Tom Lawson protested, but he was overruled by the top brass of the Coastwise Transportation Company for whom she was being built."

Captain John G. Crowley, who had successfully built the first five-master (*John B. Prescott*) as well as the first six master, had great faith in this, the world's first seven master. "Being made of steel, she will be light, fast, and inexpensive to operate," he said. "Instead of a crew of thirty or forty men, we'll need only sixteen. We will have donkey engines at the foot of each mast to hoist and lower sails, and other engines to handle heavy anchors and do stevedore work.

She'll carry more tons of coal faster and easier than any other ship ever built, and will make a lot of money."

The dimensions of this huge schooner were as follows (Bureau of Navigation, "List of Merchant Vessels of the United States" 1906):

Gross tonnage	5,218
Net tonnage	4,914
Length	375.6 ft.
Breadth	50 ft.
Depth	22.9 ft.

The other big schooners, of course, had been made of wood, but on this leviathan, the hull with double bottom, and two decks were of steel, as were the seven tubular masts, said to have been each one hundred thirty-five feet high, towering one hundred ten feet above the deck, and topped with fifty-eight foot spars of Oregon pine.

Besides the small donkey engines which raised and lowered the sails, the *Lawson* was steered by steam and had a generating plant which furnished electric light and power. Oldtime ship masters could hardly believe their eyes when they went aboard and found electric lights and fans, steam radiators and telephones in the spacious ship's saloon and crew's cabins.

For the first four years of her life, the *Lawson* plied between Newport News and Philadelphia, New York and Boston, in the coal trade, and she did make a lot of money. Then, in March 1906, she was leased to the Sun Oil Company. They shortened her topmasts, fitted huge tanks into her mammoth hull, and she entered the oil business, carrying fuel oil in bulk from Port Arthur, Texas, to Philadelphia. Again, the *Thomas W. Lawson* made handsome profits, paying her cost many times over.

On November 19, 1907, the *Lawson*, having been loaded with 2,225,000 gallons of gas engine oil in Philadelphia, set sail for England on what proved to be her only voyage across the Atlantic Ocean.

Her engineer was Edward Rowe, a native of Machias, Maine. He was the only man to have been aboard when the *Lawson* was launched on July 10, 1902 and also on board when she was wrecked. Her skipper at that time was Captain George Dow, of Melrose, an experienced deep water mariner. Besides Captain Dow there were a first and second mate, two engineers, a cook and mess boy and a crew of twelve sailors. Only two of these eighteen men survived when the great seven-master struck the ledges of the Scilly Islands off England in a wild winter storm.

I knew from the clippings in my scrapbooks that Captain Dow had died many years ago, and all attempts to locate Engineer Rowe were fruitless until, quite by accident, I heard he was living in retirement on the outskirts of Gloucester. I called at his house on October 12, 1944, and urged him to tell the details of the *Lawson's* last hours.

Mr. Rowe, then a man of seventy-two, seemed at a loss how to start. "I have never told this story but once before," he began, "and that was to the officers of the Coastwise Company." He stopped, ran his hand through his thinning hair and smiled wanly. "They were so afraid reporters would get hold of me, I was told to enter the building on a lower floor, and come up the fire escape, which

I did with difficulty because I was still on crutches. I promised not to talk to anyone, and I never have, but now, after almost forty years, and all of them dead and gone, I guess it won't do no harm."

On many things, Mr. Rowe's mind was sharp and clear; on others he seemed to be hazy, or had forgotten completely, but I have always been glad that I heard from his lips his personal account of the last weeks, days and hours of the *Thomas W. Lawson.*

It went like this.

Captain Dow was ordered to take a cargo of oil to London. The oil was worth about $70,000, but the *Lawson* carried no insurance. She left Philadelphia on November 19, 1907, in tow of the steamer *Toledo* and the tug *Bristol.* At Newcastle, she ran aground and stuck there, hard and fast, but was pulled off at the next high tide with no apparent damage to her bottom. Once free of the tugs in open sea, she stood on the starboard tack with a strong east wind.

Three days later, the wind came about, even stronger, from the northwest. "Blowing," as Engineer Rowe said, "like the very devil. We had all sails set and were making close to twenty knots."

As the wind kept increasing, Rowe became nervous, and while on the quarter-deck inspecting the wiring, he said to the skipper, "If you want any electric lights or power, you better take off some of those rags." But all they took in was topsails and spanker, leaving the six courses and the jibs. In a few hours the wind was blowing half a gale and fairly shrieking through the rigging.

The more the gale increased, the faster they went. Rowe debated whether he'd say anything more, but decided against it—after all, Captain Dow was an experienced skipper and he just the engineer.

They were off the Grand Banks and passing British tramp steamers one after another. It was now blowing hard, seemed like one hundred miles an hour, and suddenly one of the sails ripped with a terrific crack and let go, followed soon after by others.

"I can hear them yet," Rowe told us. "Boom! Boom! Boom! and away they blew, leaving just the trysail on the foremast and the mainsail."

For the first time, the *Lawson* began to ship water. Heavy seas rose, fell and smashed across the deck. Number six hatch was smashed in and the pumproom flooded; both trysail and mainsail carried away. Without these big sheets, the *Lawson* slowed down, but with such a high freeboard and such towering masts, she was still making six to seven knots. The gale, still increasing, banged against those big bare sticks and rigging, fairly pushing the *Lawson* across the stormiest Atlantic in twenty years.

Day after day the angry seas sloshed over the deck where no man could live, night after night the shrieking winds whistled through her shrouds as the *Lawson* plowed on, her captain unmindful that he was being swept far off his course.

On December twelfth, the winds died down and new trysails were rigged, but the calmer weather brought thick fog. Knowing they were approaching the coast of England, Captain Dow kept his eyes peeled for some landfall, but the air was thick with mist and low-lying clouds. An occasional snow flurry, quite unusual for this part of the world, cut visibility to zero, and the *Thomas W. Lawson,* all her seven masts bare except for trysails, wallowed on. Extra lookouts were posted, and when their trick was done, they tumbled into the engine room, glad to get warm and to drink the coffee which Engineer Rowe kept on hand.

"It was Friday the thirteenth," he said, "when I heard the cry, 'Land ahead!' and rushed up on deck. At first it looked like a cloud, but as the air cleared I could make out a towering cliff, rising sheer from the water. It wasn't more than a quarter mile dead ahead, and I could hear heavy surf striking on the rocks below. I also heard the order 'Let go the anchors!' and soon we slowed down . . . with that ninety foot wall of rock rising from the sea just ahead."

The *Lawson* was some eighty miles off her course, due to a deviation of her compass which apparently had not been calculated; Captain Dow now knew he was up against one of the one hundred forty small rocky pinnacles that make up the Scilly Isles, some twenty-five miles west by south of Land's End, England. The two ten thousand pound anchors bit into the rough bottom of Broad Sound and held; the *Lawson* slowed to a stop, practically under the precipitous cliffs of Annet Island. They were so close they could see outlines of small buildings, patches of green grass on the higher parts, and a few sheep huddled together.

Fearing the vessel might drag and be blown against the rocks, Captain Dow ordered distress flags flown and rockets fired to summon help. The sharp staccato wail of the *Law-*

son's steam siren rose and fell above the roar of crashing breakers, but the rockets, dampened by wet weather, were useless. Flares were ignited, and these were sighted by the lightship off Bishop's Rock. A call for help was relayed to all stations and two power-driven surfboats put out from St. Agnes and St. Mary's. The St. Mary's lifeboat arrived first and signaled she was coming alongside to take off the crew. Captain Dow tried to wave them off, but on they came until, caught by a giant sea, the lifeboat was hurled against the hull of the *Lawson*, losing its mast and rigging. However, a Scilly Isles pilot, William Hicks, managed to scramble aboard the *Lawson*, bringing with him a life-line.

The wind was now rising again, so Hicks urged Captain Dow and his men to slide down into the lifeboat. But the Captain, believing he could work his way out of his dangerous spot, refused to leave the *Lawson*, and his crew stayed with him. Hicks also remained on board, ordering the lifeboat back to shore to telegraph for tugs. As she left on this mission, the boat from St. Agnes arrived, but, observing that the St. Mary's boat had lost her mast in collision with the *Lawson*, she remained a safe distance away.

Just then, an Englishman named George Allen, of the *Lawson*'s crew, attempting to cross the deck, was caught by the wind and blown over the side. His head appeared momentarily in the boiling surf, then, lifted by the surge, he was thrown onto the rocks of Annet Island. Manfully he dragged himself to higher ground where he was found by sheep herders. When word got a round that he had succumbed, the local islanders knew that the crew of the *Thomas W. Lawson* were doomed, for there is an age-old legend among the Scilly Isles that for every man who dies on land there, nine others will be taken by the sea.

The hours wore on. Answering the call for help, two steam tugs had put out from Plymouth, one hundred miles away—by that time, the storm had increased to such ferocity there was nothing they could do, and they soon returned to their base.

Late that afternoon, at Annet Island, the winds reached hurricane force; trees were uprooted, small buildings were blown from the ninety-foot cliffs into the sea. Mr. Rowe well remembered that screeching winter wind, the surf dashing one hundred feet in the air, the boom and thunder of the breakers when they broke against rocky caves in the sides of the granite walls of Annet.

"It was horrible . . . horrible!" he said. "I didn't even hear the first mast when it was wrenched loose and fell. But I do recall seeing Captain Dow, Mate Libby and Hicks lash themselves to the mizzen rigging. Because I couldn't swim a stroke, I put on a life belt, and cut off the ends of the signal halyard, intending to lash myself. I unlaced my shoes and climbed onto the sheer-pole so that if the mast fell, I wouldn't be caught in the falling gear."

There was a long pause, and then Mr. Rowe went on. "The last mast twisted and crashed. I saw Captain Dow and Pilot Hicks knocked to the deck and washed over the side. Then, as the *Lawson* gave a shudder and started to roll over, I jumped, landing in a great mass of floating wreckage and oil."

"Was it terribly cold?" I asked.

"Not at first. I s'pose on account of the Gulf Stream, the

water was much warmer than the air. It was the oil that bothered me—all over everything. Thick, dark brown, smelly stuff. Got into my hair and eyes, and try as I might, I couldn't help swallowing some of that horrible stuff."

Mr. Rowe passed his hand over his eyes as if to wipe away the memory of that terrible night when he floated in the midst of oil-soaked wreckage, the thunderous breakers all around him.

"My clothes were heavy with oil, so I worked out of my coat and kicked off my trousers. Then all I had on was my long underwear and my life belt."

When I asked, "What time was it when you left the *Lawson*?" he answered promptly.

"About 1:30 Saturday morning the fourteenth of December. I saw the schooner lying on her side, looming up like a brick block, with all her lights going. Suddenly she split in two between where the sixth and seventh masts had been; the stern half grounded on the point of Annet Island and the other half rolled over and went down like a tin pie plate. My generator kept going till the very last. When the lights went out, it was now dark. And the *Lawson* was gone."

Cables from Hughtown, capital of Scilly Islands, dated December fourteenth said, "The lights from the schooner *Lawson* were observed by men on Bishop's Rock until 2:45 A.M. Saturday, when suddenly they dimmed and disappeared."

Salvage boats, arriving on the scene at daybreak, found the sea considerably quieted by the escaping oil. There was very little wreckage. A search of the nearby rocks and islands was started after three bodies were found among some rocks. And in one of the searching parties was Frederick Hicks, son of the Scilly Island pilot who had boarded the *Lawson* and remained to render what assistance he could. As Hicks' boat came round Welweather Rocks, he sighted two figures huddled between two points of rock, and instantly leaped over the side and swam rapidly toward the V-shaped ledge. Passing his line around the nearest pinnacle and pulling himself up, he discovered Captain Dow and Engineer Rowe. The Captain had a broken arm, Rowe was badly cut and bruised, but somehow they had managed to cling to this precarious shelf a few inches above the roaring sea.

In halting sentences, Mr. Rowe gave me his version of this experience. Numbed and sickened, and with his legs skinned from ankles to knees, he had floated for hours, washed along with oily wreckage. "One time," he said, "a piece of centerline bulkhead drifted by me and I grabbed hold of a spike, but it was torn from my fingers and I cut my hand. Later, I got hold of a twenty-foot timber, but I saw a sailor floundering near it, so I shoved it toward him and yelled, 'Grab on!' but he was near death; he failed to reach the timber and sank out of sight."

After this, Rowe became unconscious and drifted about until he was awakened by the sun shining in his eyes. There was solid ground under his feet and rocks covered with seaweed. He crawled onto the kelp-covered ledges, wiped the oil from his eyes and looked around. Some distance away, he saw the V-shaped rocks of Welweather Ledge, and between them, a huddled form. The waves were rolling in threes followed by an interval, and Rowe figured that if he got back into the water, he might, with the buoyancy of his life-belt, be able to reach the rock where the man lay.

Working his way into deep water, he let the first wave carry him out, but he was washed back. The second wave carried him farther, but not close enough. He tried again, and the third wave bore him near enough to the rocks so he could thrust his hand into a crevice. The pull of the receding wave on his body nearly yanked his arm out of the socket, but he held fast, and was soon examining the silent figure wedged between the rocks. Turning the man over, he saw that it was Captain Dow, still breathing but insensible.

Rowe was too weak to attempt to lift him, so he slipped his hands under Dow's armpits and dragged him higher, placing him in a sitting position with his back against the ledge. In turning, Rowe slipped and fell forward, smashing both knee caps on jagged rocks. Then, unable to rise to his feet again, he pulled himself to the Captain's side and dropped into oblivion.

When he came to, he was aware first of the rising tide lapping around his feet, then of young Frederick Hicks bending over him, and then of the St. Agnes surfboat standing a few yards out from the rock.

Telling these dimly remembered details of a marine disaster that took place in 1907 was not easy for Mr. Rowe, and at this point he repeated, "Of some things I have only a hazy memory." He did recall being taken to St. Mary's and having broom sticks fitted to his legs as splints so he could stand, and the long, painful trip to the hospital at

Penzance where a local minister brought goose grease for his bruises. Anxious to get home, although still in bad condition, he was carried aboard the steamship *City of New York.* A group of doctors from Vienna offered to operate on his legs, free, but Rowe refused this highly expert medical attention, saying, "I'll be all right as soon as I can see that old doctor in Providence, Rhode Island, who helped a painter with a broken back by inserting a piece of kangaroo bone in his spine."

He did see the old physician, who patched him up so that he could return to Boston, on crutches. Still on crutches, he reported at the Coastwise Transportation office, announced that he was ready and anxious to go to sea, and signed up on the company's six master, *Mertie B. Crowley.*

He had been luckier than the *Lawson.*

"Dug-out" Dan

IT WAS A MILD MORNING in 1925 when Larry Brown and I discovered "No. 9 Place" and first became acquainted with "Dug-out" Dan. We left Lynn before daybreak, had orange juice in Concord, New Hampshire, then drove through the fog to Bristol, stopping to watch the mist rise over Newfound Lake and melt in the morning sun. By the time we had crossed the Connecticut River into Vermont, the fog had burned away and it was the beginning of a warm, clear, bright summer day.

Just outside East Barre we spotted a roadside gas pump bearing a sign, "Hot Coffee & Doughnuts" so we slowed down, turned in and parked under some trees. Directly ahead was a steep hill, and smack in the middle of it we saw a length of stove pipe with smoke curling upward. As Larry unscrewed the gas cap, a tall, spare man with a shock of white hair and a Fuller-Brush mustache came up from the brook.

"Hain't got no gas, boys," he announced with a Vermont twang, "but my doughnuts are done and the coffee's a-bilin'. Git out and stretch your laigs."

A six-foot sign suspended between a pine tree and the chimney of an out-door fireplace proclaimed this as "No. 9 Place" and in smaller letters the sign said, "The GET ACQUAINTED CLUB for those who are lonely." Just where the Lonely Hearts headquarters was located was not apparent, for all we saw was the side of a hill covered with trees, the space where we parked, the tiny stream at one side, and out front, close to the highway, the gas pump and coffee sign.

Closer inspection showed a door and windows set into the side of the gravel bank, revealing that "No. 9 Place" if you please, was located *underground*. As we started in, we heard a clanking sound and turned to see a huge circular wire cage revolving in the morning sun. Inside the tiger-sized contraption was a small, sad-faced, under-fed, gray squirrel. His once bushy tail was between his legs, and they were not moving half fast enough, I thought, to turn that heavy cage.

"That's Atlas," our host explained, "but you don't have to feel sorry for him. He hain't making that cage go round, it's hitched to a water-wheel I got hid in the brook. He's just gittin' a free ride. That squirrel brings a lot of business. He 's one of my best 'come-ons.' Folks drive up to get gas, and get out to investigate and take pictures. Then they smell my coffee and the rest is easy."

He chuckled and hitched up his trousers. "Last fall a couple of old hens drove up and denounced me for making Atlas work so hard, and when I refused to turn him loose, darned if they didn't report me to the S. P. C. A. Fooled them all right but come in and get a cup of coffee."

The room we entered was low ceilinged, cool and semi-dark. It had been dug deep into the hill, lined with cement blocks and plastered over. A wide mahogany bar ran the length of one side, or at least it was stained mahogany, and over it a cut-out cardboard ivy vine, advertising Coca-Cola, gave a touch of color. In one corner we made out the familiar figure of the Moxie man, clad in white coat and pointing his finger straight at us. A bunch of lithographed bananas, suspended from a nail, swung gently.

Small round tables and wire chairs showed that light refreshments were served here, and several dusty palms in green wooden tubs gave evidence of more dignified social events. The most striking decoration was two trees which were apparently growing through floor and ceiling. Between them stood an iron kettle filled to the brim with business and calling cards.

"From my customers," our host explained, shoving a bony hand among the cards and letting them sift through his fingers. "Fifteen thousand cards in that there kittle. Days when it's dull around here and on winter nights when I'm alone, I like to sit and read 'em and try to remember what the folks looked like who left 'em."

He heaved a sigh and disappeared behind a curtain.

Larry, squinting at the trees, asked "Have you noticed that those trees are alike in every detail?"

But before I could answer, the old man was back bringing thick cups, sugar bowl and a plate of doughnuts.

"Them trees," he said, snapping a doughnut in half and washing it down with coffee, "are alike, twin trees as it were, and I'll bet anything you say, you can't tell which one is real and which is hand made?"

He gulped the other half of doughnut. "God Almighty made the first one, and I made the other outa Portland cement, and a hell of a job I had duplicating them branches." He tapped the nearest tree with his coffee mug and it gave forth a metallic sound. "That's the one I made. You should see the kids' faces when they try to carve their initials in that cement bark. How many sugars you fellers want? Take four spoons myself."

The doughnut I bit into was a disappointment. They were "sinkers," but the coffee was good, at least pretty good; what it lacked in bouquet it made up in temperature and strength. Our second cup would hold up a tenpenny nail.

It had been years since I had seen an oldtimer pour steaming hot coffee into a saucer, blow and then strain it through a sizeable mustache. It's no trick for a novice to try, but our host was past master. He poured, raised the saucer, blew and sucked loudly, wiped his lips with his sleeve, said, "Ahha" and then tilted back in his chair, thumbs under galluses in true Yankee style.

I produced my notebook and asked, "Tell me what made you build a place like this, underground? Why 'No. 9'? What's back of it all?"

"RHEUMATIZ!" he roared, "My back's back of it all.

So gol-durned sore and lame I couldn't stand straight and couldn't sleep nights till I met Henry Jordan. He's the feller who told me what to do and that was in August 1909 but I didn't start diggin' till lots later."

I motioned for him to continue.

"Here's how it happened. Hen Jordan had rheumatiz somepin awful. Lived on a farm and was all doubled up. One day an old Injun stalked into his yard selling sweet grass baskets. Hen didn't want none, but as 't was cold and rainy he let the Injun sleep in the shed and he gave him a handout for supper. Next mornin' the Injun handed Hen a small basket for his wife to keep her fancy work in, and on the way out he said, 'Diggum hole in ground, get in and stay there, two weeks, three, maybe six weeks. Pain all go away.' "

"Dug-out" banged his fist on the table and bellowed, "And by Godfrey, the pain did go away after Hen had been squatting in that there hole less than two weeks!"

"And then what?"

"Oh, Hen's neighbors come over and poked fun at him, but one feller says, 'What in hell are you doin' down in that hole, Henry?'

" 'Curin' my rheumatiz,' says Henry.

" 'Well,' says he, 'I gut it too. Move over.'

"Now there warn't room for both of 'em so they made it bigger, put in a board floor and a double cot, and they had a box to hold their grub and play checkers on. They was real cozy. When it rained, they covered up the hole with an old barn door, using the glass in the door for a skylight. Made a good thing out of it too. Yup! Cleaned up they did."

"Go on. How did they clean up?"

"Well, sir, folks heard two old fools was living in a hole and they come to rubber at 'em, so the boys hung a shirt over the winder and put in a piece of gutter pipe with a milk pail under it. And up on the ground they had a sign, 'Five Cents a Peek.' When they heerd a nickle clink in the bucket, they'd yank aside the curtain, look up and thumb their noses." "Dug-out" slapped his bony knees and laughed heartily.

"What finally happened?"

"Oh, Henry got better and moved up ter New York State. Dug himself a real fancy hole and stayed there for years. Wrote a book about it. Said he liked living with the angle worms. I met him one day and he told me I could be cured if I'd stay underground. That was the ninth hour of the ninth day of the ninth month of 1909, so when I built this place, I called it 'No. 9' and my neighbors called me 'Dug-out' Dan. My real name's Dana Smith, but finish your coffee, boys, and I'll show you round."

The room adjoining was larger and much darker and in the shadows we saw what looked like a small submarine. It was long and black and round, and up forward was what appeared to be the conning tower. Pipes of every size protruded from the rounded sides and disappeared in all directions.

"My heatin' plant," Mr. Smith explained. "Made 'er out of odds and ends. That boiler belonged to the Highway

Department. I found it on a dump, patched it up, built a fire box underneath and she works good."

He said, "When I close the gate in the brook, the water rises and runs into my boiler. Then I start my fire and with a twenty-pound head of steam I can make the Devil sweat. Fuel? Oh, anything I happen to have, old trees, fence rails, busted billboards, maybe part of a privy. And does she heat! Had it ninety in here when it was twenty below outside. Customers like it nice and warm, especially on Saturday nights when they drop in for a glass of sody, game of cribbage, or to dance and see the show."

"You have FLOOR SHOWS?"

Dana Smith winked. "No, not a real floor show. More of an educational entertainment. I sing, speak pieces, give lectures on my travels and play the fiddle."

"Ever show pictures with your travel-talks?" I ventured.

He almost hit the ceiling. "How did you guess? I don't have movin' pitchers, too hard on the eyes. I have my own hand-painted panoramies. Biggest and best is the Mississippi River. Took me two years to paint that panoramy."

"I'd like to see it sometime," I said, folding up the notebook. But "Dug-out" Dan wasn't to be put off.

"You shall! Right now. Give me a hand with this roll of canvas."

Diving headlong under the stage, "Dug-out" struggled with a thick roll of canvas, standing it on end and tamping hard to dislodge the dust which rose in a cloud all around us. Spiders scampered for safety. We helped him tote the roll to the stage and there it was placed upright on one side of a fancy picture frame. Gingerly he drew the loose end across the back of the frame, flattening the wrinkles as he pulled, finally fastening the end of the canvas to a slotted wooden roller.

Wiping sweat from his brow, he slipped a crank in place, flipped a couple of switches on and off, then removed his coat and hung it on a nail. Clearing his throat, he made a low bow, and in his professional "lecture" voice, "Dug-out" Dan addressed his audience of two.

"Ladies and Gentlemen, what you are about to see is the only hand-painted panoramy of the mighty Mississippi River, painted by my own self from memory about forty years ago. As the scenes unroll before your eyes, I will explain them, with special sound effects, and if anyone in the audience wishes to ask questions, speak right up."

He turned a button on the side of the frame and the room was plunged into darkness. He touched another button, and a spotlight in back bathed the picture frame with amber light. The show was about to commence, but first "Dug-out" leaned forward and whispered, "Generally I have mood music, but my phonograph broke down." Darkness swallowed him, but we could make out his white head as it bobbed up and down as he stooped and rose, turning the crank.

The amber light turned to pale yellow, and across the canvas appeared the Mississippi framed by branches of sycamore trees and Spanish moss. In the distance, a steamboat plowed through coffee-colored water. "Dug-out" tooted a couple of times, first softly then louder. Then tall reeds and cat-tails moved into the foreground and he imitated blackbirds and bull frogs, and suddenly from the wrinkles on the right hand roller, the prow of a steamboat emerged, followed by another, both boats churning the painted water and belching smoke and sparks from their tall stacks.

"Steamboat race!" yelled "Dug-out," turning faster now, and giving the canvas an occasional yank to make the steamboats rock and roll.

"*Robert E. Lee* is gaining!" he yelled, letting go a shrill whistle and at the same time ringing a bell back stage. And as the first boat floated out of sight, he shouted, "*Robert E. Lee* wins the race!"

The stern paddle-wheels of both boats disappeared at the left hand side of the frame, and were replaced by a sloping river bank covered with fields of green and golden grain, knee deep in which stood fat, staring cows. At one side, spirited horses leaped over stone walls, and in the blue sky overhead, many a painted bird paused in flight.

"Dug-out" was turning faster now, and giving forth such a torrent of bird calls, cow moos, horse neighs, and whistles-in-the-distance, we wondered that he didn't collapse.

Then followed a precious moment of silence, except for the creaking of the rollers, and the grunts of the engineer, while a lone rider, black bearded and with cocked gun, slid across the canvas.

"Daniel Boone!" shouted "Dug-out," so we cheered and clapped and it was well we did, for the next moment "Injuns" appeared, and I would not have had "Dug-out" Dan think we were unappreciative when he was giving us his best: his one-man imitation of Daniel Boone beating off the redskins while Old Man River, behind them, rolled on and on. Talk about sound effects! He had them all, not just once, but over and over, and all the time the bundle of canvas at the left side of the frame was getting thicker, and the rollers harder and harder to turn.

Our host explained that his hand-painted panorama represented twelve hundred miles of the Mississippi, and after we had seen at least a thousand miles of it slide by, we were sure he had not exaggerated. As time dragged on, and the winding became more difficult, the river and "Dug-out" slowed down. Screams of eagles and coyote calls became mere tweets and twirps, the whistles fainter and fainter, and we were relieved to hear a whispered announcement from back stage.

"The climax!"

But it was several climaxes piled one upon the other. The pale yellow light burst into a red glare, appropriate for the prairie fire which followed. Then came a cotton field with dozens of cute little pickaninnies balancing baskets of cotton on their kinky heads. For a third dimensional effect, "Dug-out" had glued real cotton onto the painted bushes, but that was forty years before, and rolling and re-rolling had flattened the tufts down, and none of them even resembled white.

However, the scene struck a responsive chord in the old man's soul, and he gave us a wheezy rendition of "Swanee River" and as the words died away, a house of logs appeared on the canvas, and in front of it some vaguely familiar figures.

"Uncle Tom's Cabin," "Dug-out" explained, reaching up to smooth a wrinkle that made little Eva even more wobbly looking than was intended. Then, as the tip of Simon

Legree's black snake whip entered the roll and wound up like a mouse's tail, "finale" was announced. Not stopping his cranking, "Dug-out" reached up and slapped another switch. A sickly green spot played across the canvas, revealing the most desolate scene imaginable. Jagged trees with vultures perched on their dead branches, stumps protruding from stagnant pools, and so many prodigious alligators with open jaws lolling around, there was hardly room for the water.

"Dismal swamp," "Dug-out" announced, "at sunset."

He mopped his brow, snapped another switch, and a lurid glow engulfed the desolate scene. Crimson melted into purple, then changed into blue, and as "Dug-out" raised his flashlight behind holes pricked in the canvas, tiny stars twinkled in the cloth sky. Now, our producer was fumbling with ropes and wires and something that sounded like an empty biscuit tin.

He whispered, "Watch the moon rise!"

He had slipped a ten watt bulb in a tin box over which a cardboard cut-out moon had been fastened, and as he pulled the strings, the moon rose in a series of jerks behind the canvas, shining through with a weird, misty effect, and as "Dug-out" used what must have been his last breath to produce the chorus of owls, frogs, alligators, hyenas and lost souls in dismal swamp, we stamped our feet (mine had gone to sleep) in loud approval.

We offered to help him roll the canvas back, but he said, "Leave it be. The children like to see it run backwards."

Now the old man was alternately beating the dust from

his clothes and mopping his face. He had given us a special show, and Norman Bel Geddes at the close of a performance of "The Miracle" could not have been more proud.

It was crude, and at times ludicrous, but into that seemingly never-ending roll of dusty canvas had gone hours of painstaking labor, no little amount of artistic skill, and more than ordinary imagination and stage craft.

Laying aside his crank, and turning off the stage lights, "Dug-out" said apologetically, "Too bad you boys couldn't have seen this on Saturday night, with music and a big audience. Goes over especially big then, when the boys are full of beer, and all of them helping with the steamboat whistles and animal sounds. Yup, she really goes over on Saturday nights, my panoramy does." And we believed him.

I picked up my camera and moved toward the door. "Say," he said in a sorrowful tone, "ain't you gonna see what I got upstairs?"

I took a long breath and followed the old chap who seemingly had endless energy, and when we reached the room above, the only one in the whole place with windows and daylight, and I saw the bed he had built, I added to myself, *and endless patience*.

This enormous four-poster and canopy-covered bed and the bureau beside it were of bird's-eye maple covered with thousands of small shells .

"Took six years to finish it," "Dug-out" said, laying a gnarled hand on one of the massive, hand carved, shell encrusted posts. "I got these posts out of a house that was being torn down. When the frame was finished, I put on the putty and pressed the periwinkles into it, and then give her three coats of shellac. It was the inlay took the time. Used thirty-five hundred pieces of bird's-eye maple and six bushels of sea shells."

The ornate and unconventional design of the inlay, and the decoration of shells would have been enough to make this bed distinctive, but that was not all. Around the top, inside the purple velvet drapes, was a spectacular frieze–I guess you would call it that–of sixteen- by twenty-inch portraits of prominent people alternated with large sections of looking glass. First there was Anna Held, then a mirror, then Teddy Roosevelt and another mirror, then John L. Sullivan, and more mirror. It made me dizzy just to look at it, and how anyone could sleep after looking up at such a combination was a mystery.

But "Dug-out" confessed that he didn't sleep there very often. "Have to stay down stairs to watch the boiler," he said, "but sometimes I come up and lay down, and I like to stretch out and look at my friends, Buffalo Bill, Jim Jeffries, and the girls in the 'Black Crook' chorus."

He ran his hand over the edge, and one of the shells came out of the dried putty and fell to the floor. "Too dry up here, and it's a pity the sun ain't shining, for when it streaks in and hits them mirrors, all sorts of colors splash in all directions, just like having a rainbow right in your bedroom."

On the way down stairs, I noticed a baby's shirt stretched on a shingle with a blackboard beneath it.

"You forgot to tell us about this. What's it for?"

With almost fiendish delight, "Dug-out" sprang across the room, and, erasing the figures *159*, he wrote *160.*

"That there baby's shirt is to make darn fools ask questions and you're the one hundred sixtieth to fall for it!"

He had amused me, and now I had amused him; we were even.

Thunderbolt

THE ONLY ROUND, red schoolhouse in New England stands in the village of Brookline, Vermont, some fifteen miles above Brattleboro, in the West River Valley.

Built in 1822, today it serves as community center and voting place. The rough unpainted benches, pot-bellied stove and sixty-odd desks have long since been removed, but the curving blackboards still cling to the circular walls, and the windows still overlook the nearby crossroads.

Why was this schoolhouse built round? Because Dr. John Wilson wanted it that way.

Brookline, Vermont, in the early eighteen hundreds was a thriving settlement. It boasted a grist mill, three saw mills and a large tannery. The stores on its single main street, and the tavern, prospered. The church was well filled on Sundays and on weekdays the children studied their lessons in three log cabin schoolhouses. Those buildings are gone, but not the round red schoolhouse designed and built for the man of mystery who arrived in Brookline just as it struggled to its feet after two disastrous blows.

In June, 1821, the crops were coming along fine when suddenly the sky was darkened by clouds of greedy locusts which in a few hours devoured nearly every green leaf and growing vegetable. Only a few farmers managed to save their grain by lashing the fields with ropes.

Two weeks later, into a clear summer sky came swift black clouds which brought thunder, lightning and hailstones, and it rained so hard and so long the little settlement of Brookline was all but washed off the map.

Small brooks became roaring streams which gouged the hill sides, carrying away top soil and leaving ugly, bare ledges and rock-filled gullies. Low lands were quickly inundated; cattle and sheep drowned. Stores and mills along the river were crushed like matchwood and the wreckage washed downstream. Many dwellings were abandoned, the discouraged citizens packing their soggy possessions and moving to higher ground. Some families loaded their household goods onto ox-teams and started West; others, loath to leave their ancestral acres, stayed on to salvage what they could.

And then, as unexpectedly as the locusts and the deluge, Dr. John Wilson appeared.

Over six feet tall and of imposing manner, he was the most striking figure ever seen in that section. From the expensive silk scarf worn high about his neck, down to his polished English boots, he was faultlessly dressed, and, being so, stood out sharply among the farmers and mill workers gathered at the Town Hall to make plans for the recovery of their stricken community.

His entrance halted all conversation.

Removing his high beaver hat and brushing a lock of black hair from his fine forehead, he addressed the town fathers in a deep, vibrant voice tinged with the accent of an educated Scotsman.

"Gentlemen, my name is John Wilson, and I'm from Boston, visiting for a few weeks in Dummerston. Hearing of the double calamity which has befallen this town, I decided to offer my humble services. By profession I am physician and surgeon, but when winter weather makes traveling impossible, I turn to teaching. Since your only doctor has left town, it occurs to me I might be of double service. . . ."

He bowed, smiled and fingered the peculiar walking stick he carried.

With two of their teachers preparing to move away and their only physician already gone, Dr. Wilson did indeed seem a gift from Heaven. A carriage was procured and he was taken on a tour of the devastated village. When he returned, Dr. Wilson issued his ultimatum.

"Those decaying log cabins are not fit for pigs, let alone for children trying to study. They are damp and dark and much too far from the center of things. Now, if you are interested in obtaining physician and schoolmaster at a single stipend, I'll stay and serve you, but I shall insist on a new, well-lighted schoolhouse of my own designing."

This was too good a bargain to pass up, and he was told to go ahead and draw up the plans—but when his specifications were presented to the school committee a few days later, they were received with mixed emotions.

The doctor's neatly drawn sketch showed a one story, circular structure with a single door and five evenly spaced windows!

Benches would line the walls and sixty desks would stand in circular rows around the stove in the center, the smoke-pipe of which would extend straight up through a conical roof. Except for a small outside shed to protect the wood-pile and shelter the schoolmaster's horse, the new round schoolhouse was to be built of brick.

"Logs," Dr. Wilson explained, "rot too easily. We will build of brick and it will last forever."

The plans were openly scoffed at.

"Who ever heerd of putting pupils in a silo?"

"Think of the cost."

"That feller's crazy as a bed bug. I'm agin such nonsense."

Thus they hemmed and hawed and argued, but Dr. Wilson was adamant, and it was finally agreed to "let him have his way, he seems so sot on it."

So, in the spring of 1822, the round, red schoolhouse was built in Brookline, Vermont, close to the bank of Grassy Brook, and overlooking the Four Corners.

Dr. Wilson installed his high schoolmaster's desk, with basket of birch "persuaders" and stout walking sticks, close to the door, and as he paced between the circular rows of desks he kept one eye on his charges inside and the other on the crossroads, always visible through the evenly spaced windows.

The handsome young schoolmaster soon became the most talked about man in West River Valley, and many were the questions whispered behind his back.

"Have you noticed he always carries that funny looking walking stick? And limps a little when the weather's damp?"

"Why do you suppose he won't ever dance?"

But most mystifying was his reason for wearing a covering high about his neck. In autumn and winter it was a warm woolen muffler; in summer a handsome silk scarf, and never, even on the hottest days, was he seen without it.

Naturally, he was invited to attend church socials, kitchen dances and quilting bees, but invariably he stayed in the background, usually choosing a seat near the door and dropping back into the shadows if strangers appeared. Rarely could he be induced to dance, and once when he tried, he stumbled, blushed and said, "I'm just too clumsy to trip the light fantastic."

He never encouraged callers and he made no intimate friends, preferring to spend his evenings alone, playing softly on his bagpipes and sipping brandy.

In spite of his peculiarities, he was a skillful physician and a fine schoolmaster and the whole town was sorry when, after a single year of teaching in the round, brick schoolhouse, Dr. Wilson resigned, moving across the river to Newfane in the fall of 1823 to hang out his shingle as a practising physician.

There he remained for twelve years, ministering to the sick, making no friends, and spending most of his time working on a new invention: an engine to saw logs by steam.

Then, without warning, Dr. John Wilson disappeared, and it was some time before the Newfane folks learned he had moved, bag and baggage, down valley to Brattleboro, where it was said he was building a house and saw mill on the outskirts of town. They were surprised to learn further, that he had suddenly married.

But it was not a successful union. The former Miss Chamberlain was dead set against liquor. They quarreled often, and when, in 1836, his saw mill failed and he lost money and began to drink heavily, she left him, taking their only child, a boy, away with her. She secured a divorce, and rumor said it was not just because the doctor drank, but because of something she had learned about his past.

Now he was alone with his collection of canes and guns, his bagpipes and brandy bottles.

Years went by and John Wilson became a recluse, wandering alone in the forest to hunt and fish, then locking himself in with drawn shades. He put strong bolts on the doors and windows and seldom was seen on the streets during daylight hours.

The few neighbors who dropped in occasionally for a nip or a game of chess noted a change in his usual robust appearance. His once black hair had turned from gray to white, his cheeks were hollow and in his dark eyes there was a constant look of fear.

The once handsome schoolmaster with his fine expensive clothes was now a hermit, unkempt, ugly and suspicious.

He got rid of his bagpipes, stacked up his books, put away all his medical things.

One day a passing neighbor saw smoke pouring from his partially open door, and investigating he found Wilson stuffing his stove with papers.

"Just some old medical journals I want to get rid of," he said, wiping his smoke-reddened eyes with a grimy bandana. "Have a seat. There's something I want to tell you, after we have a spot of brandy."

As Wilson stepped into the next room, the neighbor caught sight of a scorched paper pamphlet under the stove. He picked it up and thrust it quickly into his pocket.

Returning with the brandy bottle, Wilson said wearily, "Being a physician, I know my time on this earth is short. You have been a good friend–never pried into my affairs–and now that I'm going to die, I want you to make a promise."

Puzzled as to what was coming next, the neighbor nodded.

"When I am found dead here some day, I want your solemn promise that all these things. . . ." and he waved a thin, shaking hand toward his few possessions, "will be destroyed."

Gently touching his favorite trout rod, he said, "This you may keep, and you can have any of the tools in the shed you like, but all else I want burned."

And he added fiercely, "Especially my clothes! I don't want any coroner or saw-bones poking around my poor body, and I'd like to be buried as I am now, fully dressed."

He took a sip. "Remember, friend, I want no doctor, no minister, no undertaker! Understand?"

At the door they shook hands and the neighbor hastened home, far more puzzled than he'd been before, at John Wilson's strange behavior.

On the morning of March 22, 1847, the lifeless body of Dr. John Wilson was found in his lonely house. The neighbor who had promised to look after things was away working in the woods, and as usual in such cases, local authorities were notified and took charge. The undertaker, preparing the body for burial, got a series of shocks.

First, when he removed the scarf which Dr. Wilson had worn so long, he found a long, livid scar, as though at some time an iron collar or chain had chafed against the flesh. A bigger shock came when he saw the left leg of the former schoolmaster-physician. Under two pairs of pants, and protected by three individual drawers legs, and covered with layer upon layer of paper and strips of cotton cloth, was a completely withered limb.

On the calf was an irregular scar, as though some novice had succeeded in removing a cartridge ball.

But that wasn't all. When the doctor's boots were removed, a peculiar contraption was found strapped to one foot. Part of his heel was gone, and the homemade device of cork and wood allowed him to walk without noticeable limping. When this became known, the local boot maker recalled, "That must be why he would never try on a pair of boots in my store, always insisted on taking them home to try on."

No wonder Dr. Wilson did not care to dance!

Wilson's house was searched and a most interesting collection came to light. A dozen antique gold and silver watches were unearthed, but there was no trace of the unmounted gems which several of Wilson's acquaintances had seen him handling, nor of his pearl necklace. One man remembered hearing Wilson say, after his wife divorced him, "Well, she got most everything I had, but she didn't get this string of pearls," and then he had stuffed them carefully into the muzzle of one of his guns.

He had, it seemed, kept himself well armed, for in closets and under floor boards was a small arsenal: powder, ball, muskets, several double-barreled shot guns, a rifle or two, a brace of brass-bound pistols, and in the lining of his coats, several dirks.

When the officials came upon the peculiar cane the doctor always carried and pressed the handle, it clicked, and out snapped a long steel blade, sharper than any sword.

It is not difficult to imagine the effect of such startling discoveries on the people of the West River Valley. Whenever they met, on the street, in stores, at the mill or in church, the questions on every lip were:

"What did he have all those guns for?"

"Of whom was he afraid?"

"What kind of crime had he committed?"

"Was his name really John Wilson?"

On this last, the authorities gave him the benefit of doubt, for on the marble slab above his grave in Brattleboro's Prospect Hill Cemetery, you will find this incription:

JOHN WILSON, M.D.
Educated at
Edinburgh-Scotland
Died Mar. 22 1847
AE 58

At least one man believed that was not his name, for in the paper pamphlet he'd snatched from under the doctor's stove were the answers to many questions. This was not a medical publication he was getting rid of, as Dr. Wilson had said, but a cheaply printed pamphlet entitled:

Confession of Michael Martin, alias "Captain Lightfoot" recently hanged at Charlestown, Mass. for the robbery of Major Bray

and

A Brief Account of his partner in crime, the notorious Highwayman

THUNDERBOLT

A copy of Michael Martin's *Confession* can be found at the Vermont Historical Society at Montpelier and in many local libraries. It reads something like this:

"I was born near Kilkenny, Ireland, in 1795 of respectable, devout, Roman Catholic parents. They had five children and I was the youngest and most troublesome. Having a violent temper and a dislike for school I was early apprenticed to an uncle, from whom I stole small amounts. Running away, I fell in with bad company and being wild and reckless, I was always in hot water.

"When I was seventeen I was engaged to three young ladies at the same time and in a bad scrape with a fourth.

The police were hounding me so I skipped to Dublin, hoping to smuggle myself aboard some vessel bound for America.

"In a waterfront tavern I was approached by a man dressed as a priest who offered to help me. He was tall, handsome and magnetic with a low and vibrant voice. I went to his room and was greatly surprised when he produced brandy and persuaded me to drink with him. After we had had several drinks, he removed his cloak, and, substituting a large kerchief for his high collar, he confided he was not a priest but a notorious robber, upon whose head at that moment was a handsome price. As proof, he showed me police posters bearing his likeness.

"As he paced the room, stopping to listen every few minutes, he twirled a peculiar walking stick in which was concealed a long, sharp blade.

" 'In Edinburgh, where I was born,' he said, with a trace of Scotch burr, 'I am known by my real name, John Doherty, son of a respectable blacksmith, but as you can see by that poster, the police call me Thunderbolt.' And raising the kerchief from his neck, he showed me a long scar, caused, he said, by an iron collar while he had been chained in prison.

"I had heard of this noted highwayman many times and of his ability to change his appearance in a matter of minutes, but I never imagined being so close to him, and to tell the truth I was a bit timid for fear we would be seen together.

"Doherty assured me there was no danger and added,

'If you will stick with me and do as I say, no harm will ever befall you.'

"He plied me with more liquor, asked about my physical strength and mental courage and by the time we had finished the second bottle, I had promised to cast in my lot with this remarkable person.

"Clasping my hand in a grip of steel he said, 'We will make a good pair.'

"We drank far into the night, Doherty seemingly well versed on medical matters, and he knew a great deal about guns and girls. He announced without shame that he was married to five different women and from three of them was making a good thing. He displayed a brace of brass-bound pistols, saying, 'It is foolish to work when you can have everything you need by just taking it from those who have too much. I rob the rich and give to the poor,' he laughed, 'but I have never knowingly killed a man.'

"It was getting toward dawn when Doherty fixed me with his black eyes, saying, 'From now on, Michael Martin, you will be known as Captain Lightfoot, brother of Thunderbolt.'

"As he shook my hand we heard a commotion in the courtyard below, and Doherty, dousing the candle, peeked through the shutters.

" 'Dragoons!' he whispered. 'And they're asking for Thunderbolt!'

"Grabbing the priest's robe, he was instantly into it, then forcing a pistol into my hand he bade me climb out the window, whispering the while where to meet him an hour later."

Michael Martin's confession recites page after page of dare-devil debauchery and hairbreadth escapes. Many a fashionably dressed traveler of the Irish countryside was forced at the point of a pistol to give up, not only his watch and wallet but also his mount and clothes, and a few moments later Lightfoot and Thunderbolt would ride away chuckling over their fine new raiment and the loot in their bulging pockets.

They waylaid wedding parties to grab the more costly gifts, and they robbed fat priests of their funeral fees. They secured small boats and sailed along the coast, robbing and escaping between tides; and the horses they stole, rode hard and then turned loose for fresh ones, would outfit a troop of cavalry.

Trapped one night in a tavern, they escaped through a skylight and dropped into trees. Soldiers pursued them, and fired, and Thunderbolt was hit in the calf of his leg. Bleeding profusely, he was helped by Martin into the woods where they lay for hours while the soldiers beat the brush all about them.

That night they dragged themselves into a bog where they remained hidden for a week with only water from a ditch and the roots of plants for food. The wound in Thunderbolt's leg became infected and gave him great pain, so Martin sneaked out to the highway, stole a horse and made his way to the village where he broke into an apothecary's and secured ointments and dressings. When he got back, Thunderbolt was in agony, and under his direction, with trembling fingers, clumsily, Martin removed the bullet with his penknife.

It was days before they dared to emerge from their hiding place, but finally forced by hunger they sallied forth, stole some clothes, changed their appearance and waited for their victims to approach.

The first likely looking carriage contained three elegantly dressed gentlemen—Justices of the Court! So the robbers reined in. Thunderbolt casually asked the time of day and when the Chief Justice drew his watch the highwaymen presented their pistols, relieving the men of their jewels, watches and wallets. Then, shaking hands all round, a gesture Thunderbolt insisted upon, they put spurs to their stolen steeds and rode away.

Because three prominent judges had been held up, the countryside was quickly aroused. Extra police were put on patrol, and posters appeared in pubs, on fence posts and the sides of sheds and barns. Along with unflattering portraits were the words: WANTED: Capt. Lightfoot and THUNDERBOLT, for Highway Robbery. Reward if captured, One Thousand Pounds!

As it was no longer safe to be seen together, the rascals separated, and there is no proof they ever saw each other again. Thunderbolt sailed for the West Indies, where under an assumed name he engaged in the stone and slate business with a bit of doctoring on the side. It was rumored that he came to Boston in 1820 to look up a brother, who incidentally had moved to Dummerston, Vermont.

Michael Martin, alias Capt. Lightfoot, slipped through the fingers of the Irish constabulary, and on board the brig *Maria*, arrived in Salem, June 17, 1819. After a month's idleness, he secured employment as a farm hand on the estate of Elias Hasket Derby, Esq., but, unused to farm labor and disliking it, Martin quit Mr. Derby and went to Portsmouth, where he worked for a while at the brewery trade.

Again it was bad company that got Martin into trouble. After a series of drunken brawls and a week of wild carousing in Portsmouth, he found himself broke—and the easiest way for him to get money was at the point of a pistol.

After stopping off for a few days at the Old Woodberry Tavern in Beverly, Massachusetts, he rode to Medford, where he had been informed "a lot of rich ones will attend the grand dinner party to be held at Governor Brooks' mansion."

On the Medford Turnpike he waited until a handsome chaise appeared with a "genteel lady and gentleman" and as soon as they passed, Martin rode after them. Presenting his pistol, he demanded, "your money or your life," and Major John Bray of Boston handed over his watch, pocketbook and twelve dollars in paper money.

Martin was arrested in Springfield a few days later, and on October 9, 1821, he was indicted on a charge of highway robbery. Three days later he was tried, convicted, and sentenced to hang.

In prison, in December of 1821, a few days before his execution, he dictated his confession, hoping, as he said, that his life story would deter other young men from a life of crime. First and second editions were quickly sold out and spread to all parts of New England.

And in that same year, did Dr. John Wilson, up in Brookline, Vermont, superintending construction of the round, red brick schoolhouse, come across a copy of this pamphlet? Did it recall wild days with Lightfoot in Ireland? Is that why the schoolhouse was built round, with windows looking in all directions, commanding all roads?

And years afterward, when he felt himself to be near death, did Dr. John Wilson—or was it John Doherty, alias Thunderbolt—burn a stack of these pamphlets in his kitchen stove? Can these things be coincidence?

In the Brattleboro Public Library are preserved a number of personal articles which belonged to Dr. Wilson: eye glasses, snuff box, medicine bag, the false heel, watch, gun and stiletto cane. One of the most prized possessions of Charles Edward Crane, scholar and historian, of Montpelier, is Dr. Wilson's old brandy flask, and from this flask, each New Year's Eve, he drinks this toast: "To THUNDERBOLT, Most Notorious Highwayman of them all!"

Mrs. Hiller's Funeral

WAY BACK IN 1873, there arrived in Wilmington, Massachusetts, a young doctor and his wife by the name of Hiller. Henry Hiller had been born in Mannheim, Germany, and got his doctor's degree there. Then he moved to England and married a charming young English girl who had just graduated from a London medical school. They took a honeymoon trip to America and liked it so well they settled on Cape Cod, but after a little while Dr. Hiller felt they could better serve humanity and themselves if they were near a big city, and they came up to Boston and looked around for a future home.

The town of Wilmington appealed to them and there they settled, building a big new house of fourteen rooms near the railroad station. The name "Hiller" was carved in the massive granite steps (it is there today) and the porch which ran around three sides of the mansion was covered with vines and flowers.

The neighbors were pop-eyed when they saw panels of colored glass set in the front door and on either side of the windows, and no one in Wilmington had ever seen such wallpaper as the Hillers imported from Europe. But it was the front staircase that set tongues a-wagging. It was a most elaborate staircase with a heavy hand rail of solid mahogany, and at the foot of the bannister there was a five-foot, life size alligator with his mouth open, ready to bite anyone who tried to go upstairs.

The doctor's office was in Boston, on Tremont Row, where it is alleged no fewer than eight other doctors dispensed his famous "Elixir," a patent medicine good for "anything that ailed man or beast." And according to medical journals of those lush days, Dr. Hiller's compound was especially valued as a "revitalizer of youth and energy." It was a tasty tonic of roots and herbs, and its great popularity may have been due to its high alcoholic content.

Be that as it may, it was a favorite tonic and widely advertised. Dr. Hiller often boasted that he spent as much as $25,000 a year to tell the world about his "Elixir"—the kind that grown-up men cried for. Hiller himself spoke seven languages and he prescribed his magic medicine in all of them, and he wasn't loath to hand it out personally to anyone who was willing to pay $3.00, $5.00 or $7.00 a bottle, depending on whether it was the eight ounce, pint or quart size.

Good, old faithful country doctors plodding around the snowbound countryside with a horse and buggy couldn't understand how any doctor could get rich so quickly. Why, they said, some days Hiller harvested a thousand dollars! It was nothing for him to rake in $4,000 a week, and in those times the doctor didn't have to worry about any tax on his income of $150,000 a year!

Both the doctor and Mrs. Hiller were good spenders and they were generous to folks who had less than they. Mrs. Hiller, one of the best dressed ladies in the land, doted on hats. She had hundreds of them, and it was a common occurrence for her to say to other ladies she had just entertained for tea, "Let's drive over to Woburn and see what Miss Dannatt has for new bonnets."

She'd call the coachman and off they'd go to the milliner's. Each woman would pick out a new hat and Mrs. Hiller would foot the bill.

Residents of Wilmington described Mrs. Hiller's appearance. "She was quite regal, and always reminded one of Queen Victoria. She rode along in a bright red satin dress holding her parasol like a queen."

Others remembered her with expensive plumes and bracelets, and diamond rings which she wore over black gloves on every finger and even on her thumbs. All dressed up in her silks and satins, she would dig in the flower beds with $10,000 worth of diamond rings flashing in the sun as she pulled cutworms out of the warm, brown soil.

In the rear of the Hiller home they built what was called the "Tower House," a big wooden structure with a tower at each corner. It was intended as a laboratory for the doctor's experiments but he died before it was completed. And that brings us to the story of the famous $30,000 caskets, and the first of the two goldurndest funerals ever seen in New England.

It was not unnatural that the Hillers should have talked about the hereafter and things of a spiritual nature; that was a time when spiritualists were rampant and manifesting mediums were all the rage. This led them to think about their funerals, and Mrs. Hiller, who loved things costly and elaborate and bizarre, said she wanted a casket such as had never been seen before. And the doctor agreed that they couldn't spend their money in any better way.

Over in Cambridge there lived a very famous woodcarver and cabinet maker by the name of James MacGreggor, and the Hillers took their plans and specifications to him. The grand old Scotsman listened open mouthed as they described the two caskets and the inner boxes which they wanted built and decorated. He figured and figured and finally told them that even with the help of his four expert assistants it would take at least seven years to do the carvings, but if they would pay him $40. a week–good money in those days–he would go ahead with the job.

The original coffin was to have been for Frances Hiller, but it was the doctor who died first, on November 7, 1888, after he had sustained an injury when he was thrown from his carriage. Just two weeks before his death, one of the neighbors asked him how his casket was coming along, and he said, "Oh, it'll be ready when I need it."

But it wasn't finished when death came unexpectedly, and so his body was placed in the vault in Winchester, and the funeral was postponed until the following year.

On the first of September, 1889, MacGreggor announced

that the first costly coffin had been completed and he was ready to tackle the second one, and Mrs. Hiller announced that the doctor's funeral would be held in a few days, on September 4. She hired a special train to bring the mourners from Boston, and Lindall's Military Band to play the funeral dirge and "Abide With Me." Wilmington Town Hall was draped with flags and black banners, and a huge crayon portrait of Dr. Hiller was hung out front.

Shortly after sundown the funeral procession formed at the Hiller homestead with the famous casket and the military band up ahead. Then came two thousand men and women on foot, all bearing lighted torches, and behind them rode the old folks in every kind and style of carriage, including hayracks, and buckboards, carryalls, buggies and democrat wagons. Behind all this were hundreds of bicycles and goodness knows how many other folks trailed along in the dark behind the flickering torches.

After the casket was placed in the tomb at Wildwood Cemetery, the procession marched back to the Town Hall where a Congregational minister read a eulogy of Dr. Hiller, and then the crowd dispersed, to discuss the funeral and especially the coffin.

The cover of the casket, or lid, had two ivy vines running around the edge and meeting in the center where there was a skull carved in the wood, and coming out from the eye socket in the skull was a creeping lizard. But that wasn't all. On the ends and sides MacGreggor had carved angels and cupids and dragons by the dozen. There were bats flying over serpents and a big owl holding a tiny field mouse in his talons. All carved in mahogany four inches thick!

Inside the box, a metal hammock was suspended from the four corners of a second, inner chamber, and on the cover of this box there were gold and silver plates engraved with the portraits of Henry Hiller and his wife, and their twenty-three children (including seven pairs of twins, I'm told) who had died in infancy.

When the steel hammock was hung inside the inner box and that was placed in the outside casket, the ensemble was supported by eight heavy brass lions' paws. These were seventeen inches high, weighed four hundred seventy-five pounds and cost $100 apiece. For a whole month they had been on display in the brassmonger's window at 104 Portland Street, Boston. The whole affair stood five feet from the floor and weighed a little over two thousand pounds. They said it cost close to $30,000.

Three and a half years after Henry Hiller's death, MacGreggor completed the second casket, an exact duplicate of the first, and when it was delivered in Wilmington, Mrs. Hiller was so proud of it she had it set up in her front parlor. When her friends came to call, she would climb in and lie down so they could see just how splendid she would look when she was all laid out.

But this was disappointing; not being able to admire herself in her elaborate sarcophagus, she had made a life size wax model of herself. And she dressed it up in a $20,000 funeral robe upon which were five hundred yards of hand-made lace. In quadruple rows up and down the front were five thousand English daisies hand embroidered by the most skilled needle-women of France.

Later, when she wanted some ready cash, she hired Horticultural Hall in Boston and put her casket and the funeral robe on exhibition. Eight powerful truck horses brought the casket from Wilmington to Boston, and guarding it were ten policemen dressed in mourning, their "billies" covered with black velvet. Mrs. Hiller bought thousands of yards of black cloth and draped it around Horticultural Hall, and charged a dollar admission. But the show was a flop, and instead of making money, she lost several thousand dollars on the venture.

About five years after Dr. Hiller died, Frances Hiller's friends and relatives were startled to receive bright red invitations printed with gold ink, reading as follows:

"You are cordially invited to be present at the renewal of the marriage vows of Frances B. Hiller, M. D. and Henry Hiller, at their residence at two P. M. Easter Sunday April 2, 1893."

Just how could the comely widow renew her marriage vows with Henry Hiller when he had departed this earth years before? And why was he not referred to on the fancy invitation as "Dr." Hiller?

Here's what happened, in Mrs. Hiller's own words to the society editors of that day.

"Among my servants," she said, "there was Peter Surrette my coachman. He came from Montreal and he was always a perfect gentleman. One day Peter asked me if it was true that I was going to marry again, and I told him no. He seemed very happy, and shortly thereafter he began his lovemaking.

"'I am a poor servant,' he said, 'but I admire your womanly qualities, and humble though I am, please accept a proposal from me.'"

Well, why not? Peter Surrette was a fine man, honest and loyal. Townsfolk had seen Frances Hiller many times driving smartly down Church Street in her own spick and span surrey, behind her handsome coachman and his spirited horses. Suppose he hadn't the benefit of a college education, if he loved the widow and she loved him, whose business was it but theirs?

So they were married. But instead of Mrs. Hiller's becoming Mrs. Surrette, her husband's name was changed by special act of legislature, to "Henry Hiller," and "Henry Hiller" he was to the end of his long life. Mrs. Hiller's romance and wedding were the topic of conversation for months.

Everything this eccentric lady did was a topic of conversation, for seven more years. Then, in May 1900, Frances B. Hiller died, and the time had come for the whopping dramatic funeral which she had planned down to the last elaborate detail.

First, of course, there was the costly and famous casket, ornately beautiful, and so heavy it required ten men to lift it through the side window of the house. When they rested it on the veranda railing, the rail buckled and several men broke from the crowd to support the casket and help carry it to the funeral car which tilted and almost turned over when the great weight was lifted upon it.

The mammoth funeral car, specially built, was so high it would not go under the trolley wires, and carpenters hastily cut it down fourteen inches. Even so, it was most impressive, completely covered in black velvet, and with broadcloth draperies sweeping the curbstone. Charles Nichols of Woburn was seated in a big chair from which he drove four coal black horses caparisoned with black netting.

There was an open landeau filled with flowers, then ten hacks draped in black and drawn only by black horses, then a long procession which moved slowly toward the church through a thick cloud of dust that hung in the hot morning air.

Policemen had great difficulty in holding back the crowds which strove to catch a glimpse of the rich carvings of owls and angels and birds and snakes, and the solid brass lions' paws which glistened in the spring sunshine. They struggled for a view of the funeral procession, they shoved to enter the church, they overran the cemetery and the tomb. They ate refreshments and peered and exclaimed, and had a wonderful time. Newspapers stated that Mrs. Hiller's funeral as a spectacle was rivaled only by the County Cattle Fair which drew eager, noisy crowds from all over Essex County.

Mrs. Hiller would have loved it; she wouldn't have been caught dead with things any different!

Circus Queen

One day in September, 1926, when I was on the photographic staff of the Boston *Herald*, the Sunday Editor called me to his desk and said, "Blackie, here's an assignment you'll like. I'm sending Lowell Ames Norris up to Haverhill to get the life story of an oldtime bare-back circus rider. Her name's Wilson. She was with Barnum & Bailey and now she lives alone with a lot of cats and dogs. Go along and get some close-ups, and enough human interest stuff for a Sunday layout."

While I loaded my magazines and got a couple of extra plate holders, Norris went into the "morgue" and found a whole envelope of clips on the circus queen. As we rode along, I thumbed through them, and learned that Gertrude S. Wilson was the only child of Moses Swasey, an oldtime railroad man of means. A clipping from *Variety* was headed, "Girl Saves Babe," and local clips told of the unsuccessful attempts of the Haverhill Board of Health to oust Mrs. Wilson from the three-room hovel where she lived with a small menagerie which many citizens maintained was a nuisance.

When we arrived in Haverhill, Norris asked a policeman if he knew where "Mrs. Wilson, the circus rider" lived, and he said "If you mean old Gert Swasey, she lives upstairs in that shack over by the B. & M. tracks, but right now she'll be up at the depot washing floors."

Noting my graflex, he added, "Better watch that camera, Buddy, Gert don't like photographers . . . or cops! Last time I called on her, when one of her snakes got loose, she chased me with a kittle of hot water. She's tough, Mister, and I ain't kiddin'."

I made a couple of shots of the shack, and by that time, Gert was coming down the tracks from the depot, so we waited and watched. In one hand she carried a pail filled with mops and old rags, in the other she brandished a broom. A tattered trainman's cap was jammed jauntily over her mouse colored hair, and as she strode jerkily from one railroad tie to the next the vizor flopped up and down. Clenched between strong yellow teeth was a briar pipe and as Gert puffed, a cloud of smoke swirled around her head. Her cinder-flecked flannel shirt was open at the throat, and under a long, black, bedraggled skirt, we saw brakeman's boots much too large for her. Then she saw us!

She stopped, put down her pail, took out her pipe, spat vigorously and said, "If you guys want me to pose with my pets, you'll have to wait till I change my duds. And look-a-here, if you put it in the paper that Old Gert's going to give up her animals and go live in the Old Ladies' Home, I'll bust the two of yer right in the nose. Understand?"

Norris removed his hat, bowed and said, "Don't worry, Mrs. Wilson. We just wanted . . . ."

"Don't you call me 'WILSON!'" she snapped. "My name's SWASEY. Daughter of Moses Swasey, the first man to bring a locomotive into the North Station, God bless his old hide, and as for that pip-squeak husband of mine, I hain't seen him since I kicked his hind end down stairs two hours after we was married.

"But don't stand here in the hot sun. Come over to the house and see my little darlings. It's nice and cool in the roof garden."

When the "little darlings" heard Gert's heavy boots clumping up the stairs, they set up a chorus of yelps and howls that recalled feeding time at Franklin Park.

"Poor dears," she said, "they get awful lonesome when their Mama's away working, but God-a-mighty, Mister, I have to work to get food for 'em. You'd be surprised what a lot it takes."

We were not surprised; behind the flyspecked windows were a dozen eager animal faces, and when Gert opened the door she was all but knocked over by her furry and feathered friends. Cats of all sizes and colors rubbed around her legs, dogs leaped and barked. A parrot, minus most of its feathers, swooped onto her shoulder with an ear-splitting shriek. A mangy monkey curled a long black tail around her neck and with a vicious blow yanked the trainman's cap off Gert's tousled head and slammed it on his own.

"Stop it, Stinky!" Gert screamed. "Now damn your lousy hide, you behave! Can't you see we got company?" And then to a forlorn cream-colored kitten she cooed, "How's Mama's baby blue eyes?"

Kicking empty sardine cans and half-chewed bones out of her way, Gert clumped to the cupboard. She broke up a loaf of stale bread and scattered the chunks on the floor, poured some skimmed milk into one pan and put water in another. The room had been closed all day and you can imagine what it smelled like. We stepped out onto the "roof garden," a tiny square of tarred gravel surrounded by a sagging fence which was held up by stack upon stack of rainsoaked newspapers, magazines, and boxes bulging with last winter's ashes.

Norris sat down on what was left of a fine old haircloth sofa and I found a good, solid Moxie box. When Gert joined us, wearing a faded, flowery dress, she flopped into a lop-sided rocker, hoisted her brakeman's boots onto a chopping block, beamed, and asked, "How about some of yer smokin' terbaccer? I quit chewin' ten years ago."

We asked how her day began, and, between long puffs, she said, "I git up around sunrise, 'cause I have to be scrubbing up to the depot by six-thirty. I work like hell all day, come home, feed my animals, and then from seven till midnight, I wash dishes in the dog-cart down to the Square for my supper, and what scraps I can pick up. Folks say I'm crazy to bother with 'em," and she jerked her head toward the shack, "but I figger they're God's little lonely critters, and it's up to Old Gert to take care of 'em."

Just then a freight train thundered by, shaking the shack

and covering us with cinders. Gert grinned and waved a grimy hand at the departing caboose and the rear brakeman waved back. "I love it here close to the tracks. Takes me back to the days when my father was on the road. We had a big, white house then and I had everything a little girl could want. You should of seen the playhouse I had, with a tower and an honest-to-God clock onto it. Cost old Moses $2,000. He thought I had dolls in it, but I didn't. I had twenty-five sick cats and kittens I picked up, and I cured every one of 'em."

I asked, "What about your school days?"

"I didn't take to school," Gert said, tapping her pipe on her boot, "but I did take to horses. You won't believe it, but I was a slick little chicken then, and the best damned rider in these here parts. I wanted to ride in the circus, but Moses said no. We had a hell of a fight over that."

Seeing that we were interested in this angle, Gert filled her pipe, and told us the whole story.

On her sixteenth birthday, Mose had called her into the front parlor and said, "Gertie, my dear, I think it's time you gave up these animals and got an education. I'll give you anything you want if you'll settle down and become a lady."

Gert stamped and swore, but Moses won out, and she was sent to Bradford Academy. She hadn't been there two days before she had a pair of squirrels nesting in her bureau drawer, and a skunk comfortably quartered in her closet. She skipped classes to tend a big black sow who was "expecting," and she brought one of the newly-born pigs into English class. She achieved undying fame by pulling burdocks from the whiskers of an old goat that no one else dared to approach. She turned cartwheels over the campus, smoked a pipe, swore at the faculty, and finally smashed a violin over the head of the tutor whom Moses had hired to teach her to play.

There was a rougish twinkle in Gert's eye as she said, "Know how I got out of that place? Well, I'll tell yer. I did open one book one day, called 'Rules of Conduct,' and there I saw a solution to all my troubles. 'If any young lady gets married while attending this Academy of larnin' she'll be promptly expelled.' "

Gert slapped a rough hand on her lean old knee and haw-hawed. "It didn't take little Gertie long to find a feller willing to marry the only daughter of Moses Swasey. We was hitched at seven o'clock; ten minutes later we was fighting like roustabouts, and I knew I'd picked the wrong feller. He had liquor on his breath, and he tried to boss me around. Two things I won't stand from nobody! I grabbed him by the scruff of his neck, showed him the door and said, 'GIT! Before I break every bone in your worthless carcass.' I hain't laid eyes on him sence. . . .

"My old man was wild, but I says, 'Mose, you know him and me couldn't trot in double harness,' and he agreed, but darn his dear old soul, if he didn't up and pack me off to another finishing school. All girls of course, and the damndest bunch of sissies you ever saw. They put chalk on their faces and chewed pickles so they'd have lily white complexions. They made fudge, read love stories and had sick headaches. I hated 'em! So I wired Moses to get me out of there quick, before I busted up the place. Moses wired back, 'All right. Go to my sisters in Peoria for a while.' "

Nudging Norris with her elbow, she cackled, "Can you imagine me getting up at six in the morning to say prayers before breakfast? Them old maid aunts of mine made me practice on the pianner all forenoon, then more prayers, a little dinky lunch, and tea and cookies at seven P.M. Bible reading from eight to nine, and then to bed with all my winders shut tight. It almost drove me nuts!"

Norris nodded sympathetically. "You escaped finally?"

"You're darn tootin' I did! I went down to the depot and made friends with an old colored man who cleaned out the Pullman cars. He wasn't feelin' good, so I took a-holt and helped him. I found some wonderful literature. A whole stack of *Police Gazettes*, and newspapers from all over. One of them papers changed my whole life."

Gertie's face was all aglow as she recalled her escape from the old maid aunts in Peoria. "I found a copy of the New York *Clipper*," she said, "and smuggled it into bed, and that night I read every paragraph that had anything to do with animal acts or circuses. On one page, I saw an ad: 'WANTED: Bareback Riders and Female Animal Trainers.

"Apply in Person. Robinson Animal Shows, Chicago.' "

Gert didn't sleep much that night, and long before daylight she was up and out. She found a man who had a donkey cart, and hired him to go to her room, get her trunk, and fetch it to the depot. While the aged aunts were wondering why she didn't come down for breakfast, Gert was off on her great adventure.

It rained pitch forks all that day, and Gert was a sorry sight by the time she reached the tents of Robinson's circus. John Robinson, owner and manager, was in the ticket booth when Gertie arrived, soaked to the skin but smiling.

"Saw your ad in the *Clipper*, and here I am! Where do I change my clothes?"

Mr. Robinson shook his head. "Not so fast, Girlie, not so fast! I don't take runaway girls in my show, and what makes you think you can ride?"

"You old fool," Gert snapped, "I can ride any damned old flea-bitten critter you've got, and furthermore, there ain't a prettier figger than mine anywhere."

Robinson rubbed his chin. "You have got a swell shape, but your language! You swear worse'n my stake drivers! Well, go put on some dry clothes, and get something to eat at the chuck wagon. I'll give you a tryout after the show. But remember, I can't pay much."

"Who in hell said anything about pay? I'll work for nothing if you'll give me a chance."

That settled it! Gertrude Swasey was launched on a career which brought fame and fortune, her name in electric lights on Broadway, her face and "figger" on the biggest billboards in the United States! Under the guidance of John Robinson, she became a sensation. She was the most capable and graceful of riders, and the most daring. Like a silver butterfly, she danced daintily over the smooth backs of four white horses, while they pranced around the ring, and she ended the act with a spectacular leap through hoops of fire.

One night her Negro servant rapped on the dressing room

door. "Miss Gertie. There's an old gent with mutton-chop whiskers, tall hat and carpet bag, asking for you at the ticket office."

"Bless God," she said, "it must be my old man Moses! Put him in the front row, and I'll give him the thrill of his life!"

When Moses Swasey saw his daughter enter the ring, all slim and shining in silver and spangles, to a fanfare of trumpets and the cheers of the crowd, he couldn't believe it was his own little Gertie who used to ride her ponies in the backyard ring at home in Haverhill. And that night Gertie rode as she'd never ridden before! To the cheers, yells and whistles of the crowd, she came back and took a bow. Then, suddenly cracking her long black whip far out from the ring, she snapped her father's tall silk hat right off his head. It was the proudest moment of Moses' life!

Back in her dressing room, Gert changed quickly into street clothes, but when she returned, the big tent was empty. Moses had disappeared. Wading in mud and straw, Gert tramped from one tent to another, up the Midway and down again, but no sign of her "old man."

A wave of homesickness swept over her. A lump came into her throat and for the first time in her life, tears came. But she bit her lip, lifted her chin, and as she trudged back to her dressing room, she heard John Robinson yell, "Gertie! Look over there at the side show!"

Gertie looked. Under the flickering glare of a torch light, with his silk hat over one ear and his sleeves rolled up, was Moses Swasey, selling tickets to a Hootchy-Kootchy side show. Moses had bought the circus, lock, stock and barrel.

Now they were completely contented. Gert at last had found a place where she could lavish her affection on everything from the tiny white mouse that ran around the clown's hat to Susie, the big, lumbering elephant who lifted Gert high above the crowds while spotlights sparkled and the band blared. This was the life she loved, and Moses was happy too. He and John Robinson got along better than brothers.

One day when the circus was playing a prairie town, the tough little tomboy from Haverhill, Massachusetts, had a chance to show the stuff she was made of. Robinson's son was visiting the show, and he had brought along his baby, John Robinson Third. The little fellow was cutting his teeth and cried a great deal, to the distress of his sympathetic grandfather.

Turning to Gert between the afternoon and evening performance, old John said, "Can't you rock him, or sing or do something?"

Gert didn't like babies, but she knew "someone" who did, Susie the elephant, and Gert marched into Susie's tent with baby John on one arm and his cradle under the other.

"Susie, Old Girl," said Gert, "I want you to tend this here bawling brat. I'm puttin' his cradle right down here by your big clumsy feet, and if you step on him, I'll whale hell out of you."

Gert always talked to her animals as if they understood every word, and Susie the elephant did. Gert grasped the elephant's trunk, pressing it gently against the cradle, swinging both to and fro.

"Now, not too fast, Susie! He's just a little tinker. That's it, slow and easy! Keep your eye on him. I'll be back before the show starts."

It is a well-known fact that animals in captivity can sense changes in the weather and approaching danger, and on this sultry Saturday afternoon all the animals were uneasy. The big cats snarled as they paced restlessly back and forth, and Nero the lion lifted his great shaggy head and roared angrily and often. A sudden sprinkle of rain sent the Saturday night crowd scurrying from the Midway to the main tent, where they huddled apprehensively as the rising gale whined among the wires and tugged at the tent poles.

Flags ripped from their fastenings and sailed skyward; ropes strained and wires snapped, and suddenly the electric lights flickered and went out, leaving only a few smoky flares. The panic-stricken spectators surged en masse through the menagerie toward the main exit. In the semi-darkness they stumbled over seats, knocked down poles and overturned three of the cages. When the lion's cage tipped over, the door flew open, and with a frightened roar, Nero sprang to the ground! More scared of the crowd than they of him, the great tawny beast turned and slunk into the elephants' tent, thus far undamaged.

Gert was in her dressing room when she heard the shrieks of the crowd. She fought her way through a tangle of sagging canvas, reached Susie's side—and froze in her tracks! The elephant was rocking the cradle, and baby

John was asleep, but less than three feet away, the lion was alternately licking his chops and sniffing the cradle.

Gert seized a pail of water and flung it with all the strength she had, smack into the lion's face! Then, scooping the baby from his cradle, she cried, "Up, Susie, up!" And the next thing she knew, a strong rubbery trunk had encircled her waist, and she was high above the ground.

Gertie had saved John Robinson Third, and Susie had saved them both!

When I talked to the old circus queen on that afternoon in 1926, she said softly, "I wish you could have seen the custom-built Pullman we had. Cost Moses a lot of money, but 'twas worth it. He and I bunked in one end, and the stable was in the other. We always carried a barrel of rum and some kegs of brandy, and every night after the show I rubbed my horses down with rum and then covered 'em with two thin blankets soaked in brandy, with a dry one on top so's they wouldn't catch cold. Made their coats shine like anything!"

Gert and her horses were known to the oldtimers who followed Forepaugh's Animal Shows, Bostock's and Barnum & Bailey's, from one end of the country to the other. Even today, circus fans prize the oldtime posters, showing Miss Swasey poised on tiptoe on the backs of her beautiful horses. The tights she wears in those pictures are said to be the first silk tights ever worn by a woman performer. P. T. Barnum himself had them made for her when she joined "The Greatest Show on Earth." She was paid $15,000 for that first season with Barnum and $20,000 a year later, but she spent it all with a lavish hand: on extravagant living, on alley cats, mongrel dogs, and on any old trouper who came along with a hard luck story.

Once, she was traveling with a troupe when the manager skipped with the cash box, leaving the company high, dry and hungry. Gertie came to their rescue, but in order to do it she pawned her last family heirloom, a bracelet with one hundred forty-five diamonds.

George Primrose, of Primrose and West, was a member of that company, and he gratefully presented Gert with his favorite horse, a real black beauty. Gert kept the animal for years, and when he passed to horse heaven, she paid an undertaker to embalm him. When her dog Jasper died, she buried him in style too, in a metal casket which cost $75. And then she sat on the grave for three days and nights so that kids wouldn't dig up the casket to sell for junk.

As the years went by, Gert and her father traveled all over the country with various circuses and animal shows, then the old man's health failed, and they limited their travels to New York and Boston, playing twice a year, in Madison Square Garden and at the old Huntington Avenue circus grounds. Finally, old Moses took to his bed, so Gert stayed home to tend him and the dozen-odd cats and dogs she'd picked up around the streets. After her father died, the estate, the big white house and a sizeable sum of money, was tied up and then finally dissipated in long and bitter litigation. Gert was flat broke. To get food for herself and the animals, she washed dishes in a restaurant and scrubbed floors in the depot, and she moved into the three-room shack where we found her.

As we stepped down from her "roof garden," we looked

into the open window of the cluttered kitchen and saw on the wall a faded, fly-specked "one sheet." It depicted a wasp-waisted damsel in silk tights and spangles, poised on the back of a prancing white steed, and framed by hoops of fire—Gert, in her prime as a circus rider.

* * * *

Seven years later, in December, 1933, something strange happened.

It was cold and clear and windy, and early morning shoppers held onto their frost-bitten ears and hugged their bundles close as they braved the biting winds on Tremont Street, Boston, where the store windows, fringed with frost, sparkled with tinsel and colored lights. From inside came the smell of Christmas, the tangy odor of fresh-cut spruce, molasses taffy and popcorn. There was the sound of Christmas, too, tinkling toys and childish laughter. Somehow it made me think of a circus, and all of a sudden, it seemed as if somebody whispered in my tingling ear, "Whatever became of that old women up in Haverhill? The circus queen?"

For a moment I couldn't recall her name. Funny I should suddenly think of her after seven years. Oh, sure! Gert Swasey! I hustled on to my office, opened the mail and tried to dictate some letters. But the little "still small voice" kept on in the back of my mind.

"Why don't you go to Haverhill, and see how Gertie's getting along?"

Finally, the hunch, or whatever you want to call it, got

so strong, I said to my assistant, "George, get the car. We're going to take a little ride."

By golly, it was cold that day, and we darn near froze before we reached Washington Street, Haverhill, and the hovel where Gert had lived for so long. It was more dilapidated than before; no smoke came from the lopsided chimney, no tracks showed on the snow-covered steps. We went up the sagging staircase and knocked on the door. No answer from Gert, no barking of dogs. I pounded louder, and pushed the door open.

The kitchen was cold and empty. The winter wind whistled through broken windows stuffed with rags and newspapers, and fine snow had sifted under the door. Most of the wallpaper was gone, and along with it the gaudy "one sheet." Except for the rusty stove with a brick under one corner, there wasn't a stick of furniture. The faucet over the sink was festooned with icicles, and a trickle of rusty water oozed over the mud-caked floor from a frozen pipe. In the next room, we could see the feeble flame of an old-fashioned fishtail gas burner. I turned up the gas, and found Gert!

She was on the floor, on a feather mattress, in a pile of old bedding, breathing hard and hugging to her breast a small dead dog.

I said, "George, this calls for some hot coffee, some soup, and whatever else you think of." He ran out.

I didn't relish plunging into that mass of feathers and filth, but there was nothing else to do. I lifted Gert to a half-sitting position with her back against the wall. She was wearing an old topcoat, held together with nails for buttons and a rope tied around her waist. She still had on the brakeman's boots, or others just like them. Long strands of matted hair hung down over her face, but her eyes were bright as she smiled and whispered, "Thank God, you've come, Moses! You got here just in time!"

Then she looked again and said, "You're not my father. Who in hell are you?"

I said, "I'm Santa Claus."

Her next words were familiar and encouraging. "Have you got any smokin' terbaccer?" Then she said, "Do you believe in spirits?"

"Sure, why?"

"Moses' spirit was here last night. I was lying in the corner under the rags when I seen a bright light, just like the headlight on his locomotive, and then there he stood big as life. But when I put my hands out to him, he shook his head and said, 'Not tonight, Gertie, tomorrow. I'll come tomorrow sure and bring you something to eat."

She pawed at the tears with a grimy hand. "He couldn't get away, so he sent you instead."

I looked around for something to make a fire with, and found plenty of kindling and a bathtub full of pea coal! Gert had no use for the tub and she had forgotten about the fuel. In a boarded-up back room, I saw the old haircloth sofa which years before had been on Gert's "roof garden," and when George returned not only with food but also blankets from the Welfare Department, we moved the sofa and put Gert on it. We said goodbye for the time being and drove back to Boston.

I laid aside the script I had intended to use on the radio

that night, and wrote a new one concerning the pitiful condition of the old circus queen, and I wound up the broadcast with, "I do hope somebody will see that Gert gets a bit of cheer on Christmas Day." I had barely left the microphone when a message came from the manager of the Ritz Carlton Hotel in Boston, saying he had a letter for me, and would I come right down to pick it up.

The note was brief and unsigned. "Just heard your broadcast about Gert Swasey. Please take the enclosed and give the old girl a Merry Christmas." With it were five crisp ten dollar bills.

So, next morning, we drove back to Haverhill for the great transformation. The Salvation Army found us a woman to help with the cleaning, and a registered nurse. I gave the woman $20 and she bought warm woolen union suits, two cheap dresses, a nice red sweater and some other stuff.

A gang of boys was throwing snowballs through the broken windows when I opened my graflex. "If you fellers want to be famous and have your picture in the papers, you've got to help!" They promised, posed, and pitched in with brooms, mops and disinfectant. They scraped the walls and scrubbed the floor, set and puttied a dozen panes of glass, put new mantles on the gas burners, and when they knocked off for lunch the old shack looked pretty good.

Cleaning up Gert wasn't so easy. She kicked like a mule at the mere mention of taking a bath, but she submitted and survived, swearing all the time like a circus stake driver. When, after several rinsings, her matted crop of smoke-stained hair came out soft and fluffy like spun silver, Gert gazed at herself in the mirror and exploded, "God-a-mighty! Is that Me?"

We kept Gert in the front room while the stage was set in the kitchen, with a "new" second-hand strip of oilcloth, a white iron bed, two chairs and a table, and some dishes from the five and ten.

One of the boys brought in a small Christmas tree and carefully trimmed it with doodads and tinsel. We tacked a bright red crepe paper bell to the sagging ceiling, and put apples, oranges, a box of ribbon candy and some "ter-baccer" on the table. Gert didn't understand what all this excitement was about, but she liked it, and as we were leaving, a freckled faced tyke provided the final and perfect touch. He dropped a tiny tiger kitten into Gert's lap!

It was almost dark outside now, and the lights of the city twinkled through the frost-covered windows. From the street below we caught the sound of Christmas carols, and in the hovel that was home to her, seventy-eight year old Gertrude Swasey sat peacefully in her rocking chair, stroking the purring kitten, puffing on her pipe, and, I presume, dreaming of days under the Big Top.

The Petrified Indian Boy

One day, back in January 1871, when George Parsons of Springfield was visiting in Turners Falls, Massachusetts, he got a hankering for rabbit stew, so he enlisted the services of a hound dog named Boz, and the two fifteen-year-old boys who owned him, and off they went on a rabbit hunt.

They were working along the river bank, not far from where those prehistoric animal and bird tracks, said to be millions of years old, have been discovered, when the hound dog set up a howl; he was sniffing at a hole in the rocks and pawing away at the ground. Mr. Parsons shoved a long stick into the hole, got no results, and went off in search of rabbits. The boys, convinced by the dog's actions he had cornered something, began to dig.

The ground was gravelly and frozen, but they managed to break away several good-sized chunks, revealing a depression that looked rather "suspicious." They were scooping out loose stones when suddenly they uncovered what appeared to be a bare, brown, human foot—and that so frightened the youngsters, they scrammed out of there and headed for home with their hair sticking straight up.

Talking things over later, they agreed they'd better tell Mr. Parsons, so they did, and early next morning, with pickax, cold chisel, shovels, and a blanket to wrap the remains in, if such they proved to be, they all returned to the spot which Mr. Parsons later described as "forty rods from the bank of the Connecticut River, some six miles northeast of Greenfield, and roughly about twelve to fifteen miles from Brattleboro, Vermont."

The sandstone, once firm and solid, had disintegrated into coarse, reddish colored gravel, and Parsons had little difficulty in scooping it out a handful at a time, and as he dug, there came to light the form of a boy, lying face down in what had been, thousands of years ago, the river bed. Looking close, Parsons saw that one hand had been flattened by the pressure of the body upon it, and when he tried to lift the body, it would not budge—it was resting on a ledge to which it was firmly attached in two places, at one arm and at one leg. It's understandable that he didn't want to leave the body there, and in trying to get it free, he broke off one foot and one finger, but finally he lifted it and laid it on the blanket. The figure was covered with a thin, grayish mould, but after being exposed to air and sunlight, this natural shroud dried and blew away, leaving what appeared to Parsons to be a "stone statue" (as he called it) of a boy about six to eight years old.

He chipped away the remaining finger and foot, placed

them with the body and took his unique find back to town.

It was the opinion of those who saw it that years and years ago, this young lad had fallen, striking his head on the rocks, and had died as a result of the injury. "Then," said the local experts, "his body was covered by mud and clay which hardened, and down the centuries lime water or some other mineral solution replaced the flesh and bone, completing the process of petrifaction, and leaving a perfectly formed figure in solid stone, perfect in detail even to fingernails and eyebrows.

No wonder it caused a sensation!

So many folks wanted to see this petrified boy, Parsons had a box made, and lined with black velvet, and in this casket the strange stone figure was placed in the center of a huge circular dining table and publicly displayed in the front parlor of the American House up in Greenfield. Curious townspeople walked round and round, gazing on the strange stone face and wondering what race of humans it had belonged to.

The governor of Vermont at that time was John W. Stewart, and after examining the petrified body, he said, "Unquestionably this is an Indian." But Professor Webber from Middlebury College disagreed, pointing out that the lad did not have the high cheek bones and elongated features of local Indian tribes.

As crowds became greater, the hotel manager moved the exhibit into the big double drawingroom, and at his suggestion an admission fee of ten cents for adults and five cents for children was put into effect. It is said that the first day, Mr. Parsons collected in dimes and nickels, the sum of one hundred sixty-five dollars!

Naturally, newspapers sent their top-flight reporters and sketch artists to do highly exciting feature articles. One newspaper asked, "Had these well-formed feet, once so nimble in the chase, sped this handsome boy through the forests of New England when the Pilgrims were on our shores, or was he struck down a million years ago while chasing some prehistoric bird or butterfly?"

Pamphlets were printed, and sermons preached, on "Lo, the Poor Indian," and a well-known leader of the coming prohibition movement took pen in hand to say:

"This Petrified Boy was temperate no doubt
Quite free from whiskey, beer and gout,
Exempt from habits which destroy
The health of every reckless boy."

And it was true, the petrified lad did have a remarkably smooth skin, well-shaped limbs and head. His eyes were wide apart, and his forehead showed him to be of an intelligent race. He was (and still is!) a fine specimen of young manhood.

Nobody seems to know why Mr. Parsons disposed of this money-making attraction he'd dug up, but he sold the petrified Indian to Brooks Whitney of Shelburn Falls, for what would seem to be a rather high price. Eight to ten thousand dollars, we were told; but Whitney, touring the country fairs and exhibition halls, cleaned up. Then along came Abner Woodward with an unusual offer.

"I cain't give you much in cash, but I got some mighty

fine Scotch whiskey that I'm willing to trade for that petrified boy."

"How many barrels?"

"Oh, I got quite a lot of it . . . probably fifty barrels."

"Not interested!"

"Waal, maybe there's nearer one hundred barrel. . . ."

Would you believe it? Abner Woodward swapped one hundred barrels of whiskey for the stone effigy found on the bank of the Connecticut River! Abner had big ideas. He wasn't going to waste his time at county fairs; he wanted to play the big time. Hustling down to Boston, he hired an empty store at 104 Washington Street, and, aided by colored posters, window cards and handbills, he put "Lo, the Poor Indian Boy" on exhibition. But somebody in the home of the bean and the cod had heard about the Cardiff Giant hoax—poking an inquisitive fingernail into a crack in the petrified ankle, somebody exclaimed, "Haha! Just what I thought! Nothing but plaster of Paris and cement, colored, I bet you, with a bit of brick dust!"

An uproar followed, the police investigated; Abner Woodward was arrested, tried in court, convicted of obtaining money under false pretenses, and fined. Taking his fake petrified Indian boy, he skeedadaddled to Canada, where he took in almost enough to pay for the hundred barrels of whiskey he'd traded to Mr. Whitney.

Then, both Abner Woodward and the petrified Indian boy dropped out of sight, and nothing was heard of either of them until years later when the box containing the petrified boy turned up unexpectedly in the Sheldon Museum at Middlebury, Vermont. And there you can see it today, along with many other, more authentic, more valuable antiques. Some say it was found in the local Express office, and when no one came forward to claim it, and pay charges, it was given to Henry Sheldon, who was always glad to get his hands on anything new, old, or just different, to add to the conglomeration of Vermont antiques and oddities with which he was filling up his residence.

Henry Sheldon had led a normal, calm existence until someone gave him an ancient Roman coin, and that started him collecting coins, buttons, books, old manuscripts, photographs and oil paintings, old China and glass, clocks and costumes, furniture, guns, the entire contents of country stores and apothecary shops. He collected stamps and square pianos, violins, old sewing machines, rolls of hand-blocked wallpaper, phonographs and, in fact, Henry Sheldon gathered together anything and everything that had been invented or used in Vermont; when his house was so full he couldn't get through the rooms, he bought the three-and-a-half story brick and marble "Park house" opposite the library, and filled that up.

He lived there in two rooms, the other eighteen crammed with his glorified junk of bygone days. And everybody laughed at him.

The heyday of Sheldon's collecting was during the late 1880's, before country folk realized that antiques would one day be worth their weight in gold. And because of this, it was possible for him to amass a treasure house of rare china, period furniture, and other things the like of which would be hard to find anywhere else. And everybody says, "Wasn't it wonderful that Mr. Sheldon had the foresight to collect and preserve all these lovely things for us to enjoy today?"

After Sheldon's death in 1907, the house was left undisturbed for many years; in 1935 the directors of the museum which he had founded got busy and cleaned house. The things they found would turn an "antiquer" green with envy—enough wonderful antiques to furnish completely several rooms exactly as they were in your grandpappy's time. Step into the old-fashioned "sitting room" and you'll find a prickly horse-hair sofa, a marble-topped table with stereoscope, a comfortable open-grate Franklin stove, and everything else to match. That handsome Windsor chair was brought by ox cart from Connecticut, but as several generations of Vermonters sat in it, it was welcomed by Mr. Sheldon for his collection.

Take a peek into one of the bedrooms furnished with four-poster bed, trundle, foot warmer and a copy of Godey's *Ladies' Book* to be read by candlelight. And look at the cat comfortably curled up in front of the fire on a lovely old hooked rug. The cat was Mr. Sheldon's favorite pet, and when she passed on to catnip and cream heaven, he had her stuffed, and she's been snoozing contentedly, head on outstretched paws, for lo! these many years.

And out in the gun room, on his velvet couch, is "Lo, the Poor Indian" (petrified, or plastered) among such a collection of authentic things that he's been practically forgotten. When I visited the Sheldon Museum, Curator Earl L. Cushman and his efficient secretary, Mrs. William Burrage, brought out all the papers and documents they have pertaining to the mysterious figure. In Henry Sheldon's diary, under date of February 16, 1884, we found, in his handwriting, this entry: "Mr. Frederick A. Leland has given me permission to place in the museum the petrified Indian boy that caused so much talk a few years ago." And that's all—nothing about where he got the figure, how much he paid, nor where the petrified boy had been all those years.

It seems to me the Sheldon Museum has a real, old-fashioned mystery on its hands. What man or men first conceived the idea of making this boy and hiding him on the bank of the Connecticut River to be found by a hunting party in the dead of winter? Could Mr. Parsons, an expert carriage painter, have had a hand in the hoax, or was it the prank of some college students? Was the statue molded in clay, and then cast, or was it carved from some special composition? And how was it that such eminent and intelligent men as Governor Stewart and Professor Webber were so completely taken in as to pronounce it genuine?

Was the placing of this faked plaster figure near the location of prehistoric footprints, just after the Cardiff Giant had been found, a mere coincidence—or was it what the publicity boys would call good timing? Those questions will probably not be answered; meanwhile, "Lo, the Poor Petrified Boy" still sleeps in his velvet-lined box in the Sheldon Museum.

Gold Mine Hoax

In 1849 the most popular topic of conversation around New England was the great California Gold Rush. Yankees who wouldn't go fifteen miles to call on relatives, suddenly sold their farms, packed picks and shovels and set off in any old ship that would provide passage, for the long, dangerous voyage around the Horn to "them thar hills in Californy."

Gold! Gold, gold, GOLD! was all that people were talking about in 1849, and in May of that memorable year, Cape Cod had a "gold" episode, now all but forgotten.

I first heard of this one night at the Harvard Club in Boston, but for details I had to turn to Don Trayser, local historian of the Cape and Clerk of the Superior Court in Barnstable. Don Trayser has more facts and figures in his files than any other chap I've met "below the bridge" and to me he has been exceedingly generous and helpful.

It was a bright spring morning in May, 1949, when we tapped on Don's door in Barnstable to ask, "What can you tell us about the Cape Cod Gold Rush of one hundred years ago?"

Don grinned, scratched his head, begged to be excused and dashed up attic, returning with several of his old scrapbooks and an envelope bulging with yellowed clippings.

"It's all in here, Blackie," he said, dumping the papers on a table, "but you'll have to be careful for some of these old newspapers are crumbling."

Most of the clips were from the Barnstable *Patriot*, the Boston *Post* and the Bunker Hill *Aurora*, and from them and from notes furnished by Mr. A. Lawrence Lowell, we pieced the story together.

It began on the morning of Monday, May 7, 1849, when three well-dressed strangers stepped off the train from Boston at Sandwich depot, and from the equipment they carried—shovels, spades, a pickax and crowbar—it was evident they were bent on digging. Engaging a two-seated team from the nearby livery stable, they drove rapidly down the woods road which led to Cotuit Port in the southwestern part of Barnstable.

When they reached a certain place, one of the men jumped out and paced back and forth among the sandy hillocks, finally saying, "That's the place . . . right over there."

It was tough going at first, through the briars and sod, but when they struck sand they made good progress, and by midafternoon they had dug a hole some five feet square and eight feet deep. Shadows were lengthening and it was getting cold when one of the picks struck something solid, and the leader, whose name was Phillips, said, "Thank heaven, that's the stone I was looking for. We have found it! But, gentlemen, as it will soon be dark, and we are very tired, I suggest we go back to the village, have a good supper, and go to bed. Then we can come back in the morning and remove the chest."

As the other two were plumb tuckered out, they hastily agreed. The tools were shoved into the bushes, and the three treasure seekers climbed into the wagon and started for town.

A mile or so down the road, they halted at the home of Captain Alexander Scudder, noted for his hospitality and clam chowder. They got out, banged on the door, asked for accommodations. Perky, brisk Mrs. Scudder said she guessed she could put them up, and called for her husband. Captain Scudder was surprised to find that they not only wanted supper, breakfast and a place to sleep, but they wanted all this in one room, with a sturdy bolt on the outside of the door, and two oil lamps which would burn all night.

The horses were taken to the stable, the men were led to the big front chamber, and supper was taken to them on trays. Around eight o'clock the Captain himself slid the heavy bolt which locked them in, and in a short time all three were snoring lustily.

When the Captain went to awaken them at daybreak, and unlock the door, the oil lamps were still burning; he was very curious about this strange procedure, but he asked no questions. Again they ate from trays brought up from the kitchen; then, while one of the men paid the bill, the other two brought out the horses and hitched them to the wagon.

With no word of explanation, the mysterious three drove out of the yard as the sun burned through the fog bank over the Barnstable marshes.

A few hours later, just before train time, two of the strangers drove into the livery stable, told the stableman they were through with the team, paid the charge, and limped wearily toward the depot. Naturally, the stableman wondered why they were so solemn, why their clothes were so bedraggled and muddy, and what had become of the third member of the trio. When the train puffed into the station, they got on, and, according to the conductor, they sat huddled dejectedly in the smoking car all the way to Boston.

A week . . . then ten days, went by, and then on the front page of the Boston *Post*, this advertisement appeared:

> REWARD OF $100.00
>
> will be paid for information concerning the whereabouts of WILLIAM PHILLIPS, alias William Phelps also known as William Porter, who two weeks ago escaped from the State Prison at Charlestown, Mass.

I might say that the missing Mr. Phillips was a notorious burglar who had stolen some "hardware" from the State Arsenal in Boston, and had been caught in the act of robbing a jewelry store in Lynn. The term "escaped" was used rather loosely in the advertisement, for Mr. Phillips (or

Phelps, or Porter) was the leader of the Cape Cod digging party, and his two companions had been none other than City Marshal Nichols of the Charlestown Police Department and Warden Robinson of the State Prison!

It didn't make sense that the City Marshal of Charlestown and the Warden of the State Prison should be sweating like laborers as they dug into the sand while a notorious criminal gave orders, until Mr. Trayser explained.

It seems that William Phillips was a good-looking cuss, and had convincing ways; maybe I should say "taking" ways, for wherever he happened to be, things seemed to get stuck to his fingers. Previous to being jailed for robbing the Lynn Jewelry store, he had lived a carefree life on an old house-boat, drifting up and down the Charles and Mystic Rivers, going ashore mostly at night—to swipe various garments from family clothes lines, and table and bed linen spread on the lawns to dry. He had raided several small shops in Chelsea, broken into stores in Malden and once he was caught red-handed while trying to force the lock of a storage shed at the Magoon & Turner's Shipyard.

Slapped into jail, Phillips told his lawyer, "I know where there is a lot of gold cached away, but I can't get it alone." And he suggested that if Attorney Jones would "make a dicker" with the authorities to drop the charge of breaking and entering in the night time, he would take them to where BIG MONEY was hidden. Lawyer Jones didn't believe this story, so all that winter Phillips languished behind the bars in Charlestown. With the first warm days of spring, he got itchy, and wanted out, so he sent a note to the warden asking for an interview. Phillips confessed that he had robbed a bank at Wheeling, Virginia, and had hidden $50,000 in gold among the sand hills of Cape Cod, and he concluded with, "If you don't believe me, Warden, I suggest you telegraph the president of that bank and see what he has to say."

Warden Robinson, thinking it would be a feather in his cap and also rewarding, should he find the missing money, did wire the Wheeling bank, and three days later the president arrived in Boston.

Phillips, brought face to face with the southern banker, told such a convincing story of his implication in the robbery that Warden Robinson, ignoring all provisions of the law, took him from prison, and, with City Marshal Nichols in company, set out for Barnstable, on Cape Cod.

Well, after a hearty breakfast at the Scudder place, the trio drove to the pit they had dug the day before, and Phillips, being always a polite and thoughtful thief, suggested that City Marshal Nichols jump in to have the thrill of uncovering the chest, while he and the warden watched from above.

Nichols peeled off his coat, slid into the eight-foot pit, spat on his hands and punched the crowbar onto the rock he had located the night before. Robinson stood peering down while Phillips gave directions.

As the City Marshal bent over to loosen and lift the stone, which Phillips said was "on top of the money chest," Warden Robinson suddenly slipped (or was he pushed?) and fell headlong into the hole. A lot of loose sand tumbled on top of him, and Phillips lit out through the woods toward the Indian village of Mashpee.

No wonder those two police officials looked crestfallen when they took the train from Sandwich that morning. They didn't mind the time and money they had spent, or the blisters they had—what bothered them most was WHAT the Boston papers would say . . . and that is why the reward notice in the Boston *Post* read, "escaped from State Prison."

But reporters did a lot of questioning about Phillips' "escape" from Charlestown, and finally the fat was in the fire. Overnight, the hastily dug pit in Cotuit became the "Cape Cod Gold Mine." Folks who only half-read, or half-heard, about the incident, believed that gold actually had been discovered, and, as the rumor spread, they came a-running, armed with spades and shovels to stake out a claim.

The Barnstable *Patriot*, with tongue in cheek, said editorially, "Since the Charlestown and Cape Cod Gold Company commenced operations at Cotuit, business has been revived locally, and within the past week, a boat with paddle wheels, along with a scow, has been launched from the shipyard. There is good reason to believe that City Marshal Nichols and Warden Robinson found only part of the buried treasure, and these new boats will be used to take away the balance."

After this came out in print, you can see why the local stores and taverns did a rushing business. It has been estimated that at least five thousand spectators came to Cotuit just to look at that hastily-dug hole in the ground.

The two officials were unmercifully kidded; Boston papers poked so much fun at them, their careers were practically ruined and their lives made miserable, while, on the other hand, clever, crooked Phillips was almost a hero.

What became of him? Well, here's the story he told. "After Warden Robinson lost his footing and fell on top of Marshal Nichols, and the two of them were floundering helpless in the sand, I ran toward the team, but finding a foot path, I followed it and eventually reached Mashpee where I was taken in by some friendly Indians. I stayed with them for a few nights and then went to the shore in Sandwich. A man named Sproule sold me a small boat, and with favorable wind I sailed to Lynn, took the train to Portsmouth, New Hampshire, and went on to Newmarket where I secured employment as a farm hand. Eventually, I wound up in a shipyard in Bath, Maine, where I got a good paying job."

Phillips confession continues, "When I had saved considerable, I worked my way back to Boston intending to find my wife and give her some money. But she had moved so I went to a boarding house in the South End. There I was recognized by my landlady, Mrs. Sweeny, and she notified the police."

William Phillips was arrested as he stepped from a fruit store, by Officer Warren, and as he was marched down Tremont Street in handcuffs, a crowd collected and cheered the "Cape Cod Miner" for having played a good joke on the officials. Back in his cell, Phillips readily admitted that the story of the buried money from the Wheeling bank was "just made up" from newspaper accounts he had read, and he further admitted that as the warden had stepped to the brink to get a better look, he did give him a bit of a shove, but he denied stopping to shovel sand and rocks on top of the two surprised and bruised officers.

The Boston *Post* said, "Out of respect for the skill with which Phillips effected his escape, there is a strong feeling of regret that he has been recaptured." And, would you believe it? more than two hundred citizens signed a petition for that scoundrel's release. In spite of that, Phillips stayed in State Prison until he had served the eight and one-half years of his original sentence.

Today, there's a mere trace of the hole in the sand, just off the old Post Road in Cotuit, where $50,000 was not buried.

Sea Water Gold

LATE IN THE AFTERNOON of a cold, raw day in February 1897, the Reverend Prescott F. Jernegan paced impatiently on the platform of the Providence railroad station; he had just come up from Florida and he minded the stinging cold. He kept tapping his thinly gloved hands against his topcoat, fingering the outline of a bottle in his pocket. As he waited for the incoming train, he wondered if the two friends he was meeting had brought their bottles, and the box which he had designed for their unusual experiment.

When the men from Connecticut stepped off the train, clad in fur coats, earmuffs and mittens, they did have the strange box, all wrapped up, and besides that they carried a heavy basket, a lantern and two small oil stoves. Mr. Jernegan helped them stow this stuff in his sleigh, picked up the reins and drove them at fast clip out of Providence proper and down toward the waterfront.

There he hitched the horse under a shed and lighted the lantern. The two men from Connecticut picked up their bundles and followed their former pastor over a long, rickety wharf that jutted into the harbor. On the end of the pier, high above the ocean, was a small shack; Jernegan unlocked the door and they went in. It was dark, windy and bitter cold. Except for a small table upon which rested some storage batteries and wires, and a couple of broken chairs, the room was empty. The one tiny window was heavily curtained, and the trap door in the floor was bolted.

When the oil stoves were going good, Jernegan took off his gloves and placed on the table the small glass-stoppered bottle which he had brought.

"All you have to do," he said, "is to put your quicksilver in the box and then add the chemicals from this vial, close the cover, attach the wires from this battery and lower away.

"I'll come after you as soon as it's daylight. And, oh yes!" he smiled, "don't forget to throw the switch! Well, good night, gentlemen. And good luck!"

A moment later Prescott Ford Jernegan (whose name was soon to be headlined in newspapers all over the world) was in his sleigh driving toward his Providence hotel. His friends, meanwhile, were preparing their great experiment. They had brought with them from Connecticut the box carefully constructed according to specifications furnished by Jernegan. It was made of wood and lined with zinc, and the cover had several large holes so that water could flow in and out.

They dumped into the box the contents of three bottles

of quicksilver which they themselves had purchased, added the chemicals left by Jernegan, attached the wires, closed the cover, and opened the trap door in the floor. A blast of cold, damp air rushed into their faces. The tide was rising and a few small ice cakes bumped against the slimy pilings beneath them.

Slowly and cautiously they lowered the box into the ocean, closed the trap door, turned on the switch, and then settled by their oil stoves for a long, cold, anxious night of waiting.

I want to say right here that no two finer Yankees ever lived than those two. They were intelligent, generous, God-fearing gentlemen, and their word was as good as their bond. Arthur B. Ryan was a successful jeweler and deacon of the First Baptist Church in Middletown, Connecticut. He had helped Jernegan get his first pastorate after graduation from the Newton Theological School, and he had been very much upset when the parishioners in Middletown objected to Jernegan's high-handed method of preaching and forced him to resign.

Jernegan's next church was down in Deland, Florida, and he hadn't been there long when he wrote Mr. Ryan a very surprising letter. It went something like this:

"My Dear Deacon Ryan: A few nights ago I had a dream during which it was revealed to me that GOLD can be extracted from the ocean by passing a current of electricity through chemically treated quicksilver. The dream was so vivid, I tried the experiment in a small way, AND IT WORKS!

"Now if we could get someone to finance a factory for

doing this work on a big scale, we would soon be millionaires."

Ryan, being an expert jeweler, knew a lot about gold, quicksilver, acids, etc., and he found by consulting his encyclopedia that in every ton of sea water there is an infinitesimal amount of gold, silver, and other metals. Roughly one-half grain of gold to each ton of ocean water.

Ryan also knew that for centuries scientists had been trying to find some inexpensive method of getting that gold out of the ocean. And here was a letter from his protegé Prescott Jernegan, claiming the secret had been revealed to him in a dream! If this exciting news had come from some men, Ryan wouldn't have given it a second thought, but this was a young man whom he knew personally and respected. Jernegan belonged to one of the oldest and finest families on Martha's Vineyard. He had been graduated with honors from Brown University, and he was an ordained Baptist minister.

If the Reverend Mr. Jernegan said he could get gold out of the ocean, that was all Deacon Ryan wanted to know. He took into his confidence Andrew N. Pierson, founder of the world's largest greenhouses in Cromwell, Connecticut, and wrote Jernegan to come up from Florida and put on a demonstration.

And that is how Arthur B. Ryan and his wealthy friend "Andy" Pierson happened to be huddling over those two smoky oil stoves in that shaky, shivery shed on the Providence waterfront in February, 1897.

When dawn came the next morning, the two half-frozen victims opened the trap door. The rope and wires were encased in ice for it was several degrees below zero. They had barely hoisted the box up and got it open when Jernegan arrived to drive them back to the city. They found that some of the quicksilver had mysteriously leaked out, but there was enough to fill one bottle, and when this had been sealed and safely tucked in Pierson's pocket, they left the shack and drove to Jernegan's hotel for a good, hot breakfast.

All during the meal, Jernegan kept impressing them that they had built the box in Connecticut and brought their own quicksilver, and he added, "And you know, gentlemen, that I haven't the faintest idea which chemist you have chosen to analyze your mercury."

All of which was true! So after breakfast, Ryan and Pierson went to a laboratory that Pierson had picked, and Mr. Ryan did the talking.

"How long will it take," he asked the chemist, "to find out if there's any copper or silver or gold in this quicksilver?"

The chemist shook the bottle and said, "Oh, better give me till tomorrow noon. Takes quite a while to make a complete test."

So they left the quicksilver and drove back to the hotel to talk things over and to rest.

Wholly unknown to Ryan and Pierson, another friend of Jernegan's was also resting in the same hotel. He was Charles E. Fisher, former floor-walker in a Brooklyn, New York dry goods store, but more recently employed as a deep sea diver. He too had been busy the night before on the Providence waterfront!

When the chemist reported the next day that he had found "quite a bit of zinc, a trace of copper, a few cents' worth of silver, and GOLD TO THE AMOUNT OF $4.50" Ryan and Pierson all but fainted! But Jernegan didn't seem surprised at all, and for good reason—he knew how the gold got in that box! He just smiled benignly.

"If one small box and a bit of mercury can accumulate almost $5.00 in pure gold from the ocean in a single night," he said, "just think what we could do with, say, one thousand of those little boxes!"

They did think about it. In fact, they couldn't think about anything else! But before they said anything to their friends about investing money to build a factory, they demanded other demonstrations and Jernegan staged them with the same astounding success. Tests were held in Rhode Island and in Connecticut, and one very promising demonstration was conducted on the desolate shores of Block Island. While the amount of gold varied in these tests, there was always more than enough to warrant going after it in a big way.

Each time, Jernegan furnished the magic chemicals which he said, "did the trick," and although Fisher, the floorwalker, was never seen, Charlie was there in his diving suit, walking on the floor of the ocean, and "salting" the box.

And so it came about that on the fifth of November, 1897, a group of excited business men met in Levi Turner's law office on Exchange Street, in Portland, Maine, to form a corporation "to get gold out of the ocean." With the exception of Fisher, who had suddenly appeared on the surface as a dear old friend of Jernegan's, every one of those men was outstandingly successful in his particular field of business, and many of them were prominent members of the Baptist Church.

Jernegan had a slick-sounding name all picked out for his new enterprise. "We'll call it the Electrolytic Marine Salts Company," he said, "and I think, Gentlemen, we should capitalize it for ten million shares at a par value of one dollar a share."

The directors agreed, the papers were signed, and each director purchased one share of stock. The remaining nine million, nine hundred ninety-nine thousand, nine hundred ninety-five shares were made available to Jernegan and Fisher who were to hire agents to sell the stock to the public. The officers of the newly formed ten million dollar corporation, with five dollars cash on hand, were as follows: President, Arthur B. Ryan; Vice President and General Manager, P. F. Jernegan (he had dropped the "Reverend" by this time); Assistant General Manager, Charles E. Fisher; Treasurer, W. R. Usher; and clerk, A. P. Sawyer. These last two were respected business men of Newburyport, Massachusetts. Andrew N. Pierson of Cromwell, Connecticut, who is said to have kicked in twenty-five thousand dollars to start things going, was made manager of construction.

When the directors of the Electrolytic Marine Salts Co. asked Jernegan where the first plant was to be erected, he had the answer ready. "Brother Fisher and I," he said, "have made extensive explorations, and we have found an ideal location on Passamaquoddy Bay at North Lubec, Maine. The tides are very high up there, and they will furnish us with millions of tons of gold-bearing sea water. Then too, the natural isolation of that section of Maine is greatly to our advantage. With a secret process like ours, we can't afford to have inquisitive competitors poking around."

You bet your boots they couldn't have anyone poking around! And the first thing they did after they took over the old Comstock Grist Mill at North Lubec was to build a board fence ten feet high all around their property, with three strands of barbed wire on the top. And they armed the guards at their "Klondike" Plant with rifles and shot guns.

But let us go back a bit and see what sort of goings-on there were up in Maine. One day in October, 1897, Hiram Comstock of North Lubec, said to his neighbor Mr. Cummings, "Bill, who's that feller in the Prince Albert, moochin' round the mill pond? Wonder what he wants?"

"Dunno," said Cummings. "Let's go find out."

The slick-looking stranger in the tall silk hat turned out to be our friend Jernegan, and before two shakes of a lamb's tail, he talked Comstock and Cummings into selling him their tide water grist mill, the pond on which it stood, and a lot of other shore property.

Then Jernegan took off for St. John where he offered Allston Cushing $10,000 for his saw mill if he'd move it down to Lubec and get it going in two weeks. Cushing had hardly caught his breath when Jernegan added, "And we'll need a lot of logs for lumber and piling. Can you deliver, say, about eight million feet of logs right away?"

"Why, er . . . . I could if we had a tug, but eight million . . . that's a lot of lumber."

"You haven't any tugs? Telegraph New York! Buy a tug! Get those logs to North Lubec!"

Aladdin himself couldn't have caused any more excitement than did Prescott Jernegan. Over night, an army of engineers, surveyors, chemists and carpenters swarmed into Lubec, followed by five hundred laborers who toiled all day or all night depending on the tide. They dug ditches, laid pipes and strung wires. They built bunk houses, bridges and big heavy bulkheads to hold back the powerful tides of Passamaquoddy Bay. As they worked, they sang, songs which the natives couldn't understand. Nor could the Lubeckers understand why a ten foot fence was put up, with wicked barbed wire on top.

When the old machinery in the Comstock Mill had been torn out, and a new dynamo installed, the first electric lights ever seen in that section of Maine twinkled all through the foggy nights as six-foot strangers armed with shotguns patrolled the entire property.

The one question on everyone's lips was, "What they doin' down to the mill pond?"

Nobody knew, except Jernegan and his closest friends, and they didn't talk until the first gold nugget came a-gleaming from the laboratory at North Lubec. Then they talked plenty, through full page ads in the newspapers and a very promising prospectus. The gist of it was that gold was being commercially obtained from sea water for the first time in history. To carry on this business there was a newly-formed corporation named the Electrolytic Marine

Salts Company, but that was too hard to remember and pronounce, so folks just called it "The E. M. S." or "Jernegan's Gold Company."

In short order, several large basins were built, and a seven hundred foot dam put in, with automatic gates to control the "gold-bearing sea water." Under the old grist mill was a sluiceway, and to this were attached two hundred and forty-three magic boxes.

When the contents of these "accumulators" were analyzed by the U. S. Assay Office in New York and found to contain gold at the rate of $308.61 worth every twenty-four hours, the rush to invest was on. The Reverend Mr. Arrington, who was also the company chemist, molded some nuggets into a "gold brick," and when that was shipped to the Boston office of the E. M. S. Company at 53 State Street, so many folks jammed in that police were called to maintain order. And a good many of the credulous who came to look, bought sizable blocks of stock at from fifty cents a share to a dollar and a half.

And I regret to say that many, many shares were sold at Tremont Temple, Boston, and at other Baptist strongholds throughout New England.

A prominent Faneuil Hall market man heard about gold being taken from the ocean, and got all excited. He rounded up a party of Greater Boston business men, and took the boat for Eastport to see how it was done. They were dumbfounded to find so many other business men down there for the same purpose. Bankers, doctors, lawyers from Boston, Providence, Hartford, New York.

When these men visited North Lubec, they saw acre

after acre of shore property covered with piling and lined with sluiceways. The old rickety wooden bridge was being replaced with an iron structure; new offices, stables and cottages were going up fast, and officials of the company had already purchased several fine year-round residences to live in. The very air was electric with the ring of hammers, saws, drills and chugging pumps—and excitement.

President Arthur B. Ryan told the out-of-state visitors, "The new plant we propose for the Canal will cost ten times as much as this. At present, we have two hundred forty-three machines working here—and each one collects about $1.27 worth of gold out of the ocean every twenty-four hours. Mr. Jernegan estimates the new plant will yield $5,000. in gold at every turn of the tide. And we have other sites in mind along the coast."

Mr. Pierson, the florist from Cromwell, Connecticut, was also enthusiastic. "I've put everything I've got into this," he said. "It's the most wonderful thing I ever heard of." And from where he sat, it was!

As a parting privilege, the prospective buyers were taken into the laboratory where Mr. Arrington was busy boiling down residue from the "accumulators." That poor man was so completely fooled by what he found, he invested all he could scrape up.

Mr. Shanahan, the contractor from Portland, was another victim. He told visitors, "When Mr. Jernegan and Mr. Fisher offered me the job as boss contractor, I said, 'I'll take it for $300 a month and board and room, and I'll match your $300 in wages with $300 of my own money, and every month I take $600 worth of E. M. S. stock. That's how good I think it is!"

Is it any wonder the investigators returned to Boston and bought tens of thousands of shares of stock in Jernegan's Gold Company? And so did thousands of other folks, many who could ill afford to speculate even a dollar in such a preposterous scheme.

But there came a day in July, 1898, when there was no gold in the "accumulators" for Mr. Arrington to make into bricks!

The reason? Well, there was no Charles Fisher to put gold into the boxes when no one was watching. Fisher, it seems, had gone away without telling anyone he was going, and then . . . . Jernegan also disappeared!

They had been away often on business. Jernegan made frequent trips to New York to confer with various bankers, while Fisher had to traipse all over the country to get old gold–stick pins, wedding rings and discarded gold watch cases–that could be melted down for him to put in the "accumulators" under the cover of darkness. This time, it was different! Nothing was ever heard of Fisher from that day to this, but Jernegan made the headlines in a big way.

He had deposited sizable sums of money in the Fourth National Bank of New York, and the King's County Trust Company, and two days after he made the deposits he wanted the money back. "To buy platinum wire," he said. The New York bank officials got suspicious and telephoned the National Shawmut Bank in Boston to ask about Jernegan's credit. It was o.k. so they gave him $90,000. Jernegan bought a lot of Government bonds, the rest he kept in ready cash.

Then the New York bank put Pinkerton men on Jernegan's trail and located him in the office of the French Line, buying a ticket to Europe under the alias of "Louis Sinclair."

On July 23, 1898, Jernegan sailed for France with his wife, little son, and about $100,000. Soon afterwards, Ryan received a letter mailed in New York. It read, "Fisher has disappeared with the formulas. I'm afraid he has fooled us all, and I'm going to Europe to try to find him." It was a dark day for Ryan when he received that news, and for several days neither he nor Pierson could bring themselves to believe they had been completely and cleverly hoaxed. Then a fateful telegram from New York authorities confirmed Jernegan's flight "under a cloud."

Foster Reynolds, the man who handed Pierson the telegram, said afterward, "Poor Mr. Pierson, he raised his hands to heaven and cried, 'What have we done! It can't be true . . .' "

But it was, and immediately everything stopped at the works in North Lubec. There was enough money in the Eastport bank to pay off all the workmen; directors of the E. M. S. Company attached Jernegan's bank accounts in Boston, then sold all the buildings and machinery, and when the last payment was made, stockholders realized about thirty-six cents on the dollar—not nearly as bad as it might have been. But Pierson and Ryan had lost heavily, and for that matter, so had hundreds of other investors. The mayor of a Massachusetts town, who had encouraged his friends to buy stock, made up all their losses out of his own pocket, and died a poor man because of it.

When the assets of the Electrolytic Marine Salt Company were finally counted, they included a most unexpected donation from abroad: Prescott Jernegan himself returned about $85,000. Heaven knows why, unless he was repentant, because the money he took away was technically his. The company had voted to pay him forty-five per cent of gross sales of stock, for the use of his secret process! And that was all he had taken!

If you are one of those who like to know "what happened afterward," let me point out that in the later years of his life, Jernegan served his country well in a most conservative capacity. When the United States Government advertised for teachers to go to the Philippines after the Spanish-American War, Jernegan volunteered, and proved a fine educator. Later he was promoted, and sent to the Hawaiian Islands, where he held an important post in educational work for many years. After he retired, he came to California, I am told, and I understand that he died there.

Some hard-hearted wag, just after the bubble burst, concocted a little jingle:

> Jernegan!
>   Return again!
> Make the fake
>   Earn again!

But he didn't, and he couldn't, and it's my belief that the ocean will not give up its gold in my time, nor in yours.

Palestine Pilgrimage

ALONG THE NORTHEAST SECTION of the Maine coast, just after the Civil War, the roads were narrow, rutted, and blocked with mud or snow for several months of the year. Only occasionally did a traveler come in from the outside world. The arrival of a Boston paper by stagecoach or mail packet, or the docking of a ship, was a big event. The natural isolation of such towns as Jonesport, Indian River and Addison tended to make each town a compact separate group, and on the subject of religion all these good, God-fearing folks agreed: the Sabbath was a day of sincere, devout worship. They put on their best Sunday clothes and sat for long, uncomfortable hours on hard seats, listening to dry, long-winded sermons whenever an itinerant preacher came to town.

It is not surprising then, that when George Joshua Adams showed up, the Down Easters should take notice.

Parson Adams arrived in Jonesport as if borne on a magic

carpet. No one saw him step out of the stagecoach or come walking up from the wharf. He just landed: tall hat, long coat with tails, and the mannerisms of an old-fashioned Shakesperean actor. His voice was vibrant and commanding, his eyes deep set. He made an instant and profound impression on the country folks. He had just been kicked out of the Mormon Church in Independence, Missouri, for conduct unbecoming a minister (probably because he was addicted to rum) but the Jonesport people didn't find out about that until too late.

Adams knew what he was doing all right when he picked that particular section of the Maine coast where simple, honest folks took their religion seriously. Cleverly and carefully, he went around the countryside, visiting each church in turn and watching the reaction of the congregation, and the effect of his sermons. Invariably he attracted a big crowd. In the village of Jonesport he sensed an undercurrent of antagonism, so he moved over some three miles to the tiny village of Indian River, where there was a small white church and a cluster of farm houses.

This is the town that he desolated.

One warm Sunday morning in the spring of 1865, when the Indian River church was packed to capacity, Parson Adams dramatically entered the pulpit with a strange look upon his pale face. His long hair stood on end as if charged with electricity. His thin lips were more tightly drawn than usual around his big mouth and his dark eyes fairly blazed with excitement. He had seen a vision! He said that an angel had visited him in the dark of night and had told him he was to lead a band of faithful followers to Palestine to open up that land of milk and honey for the oppressed Jews, and in return for their labors, and their foresight, they would receive "all the riches that Heaven could bestow on them."

He lowered his voice, flung his long arms toward the astonished congregation and said, "The Angel told me that you, and you, and you have been chosen for this holy mission. We will all go to Palestine together to work for and with the Lord! It is a miracle come true! Glory Hallelujah!"

When the stunned and bewildered parishioners left their church, they didn't know the spell that was on them. But Indian River, Maine, was never the same again. That was the beginning of the end.

On the following Sunday, the roads were black with top buggies and wagons of every description. Families got up before daylight to pack lunch boxes and feed the hens. They ploughed through mud and forded swollen streams in order to get a front row seat.

Long before the sweet notes of the old-fashioned organ came drifting through the open windows, every pew was filled. Scores stood up while the children sat on the floor. Outside on the fresh green lawn solemn-faced farmers and fishermen cocked their heads to catch the ringing words of the impassioned Elijah, more eloquent than ever before. You could have heard a pin drop in that little church in Indian River when Parson Adams cast his hypnotic eye from one honest face to another and announced his second vision.

"The Lord," he shouted, "is pleased that so many of you are ready to serve Him."

After a magnetic silence that held his new-found disciples

enthralled, he announced, "Almost within the hearing of my voice a great new ship is building, that will carry us to the far, fair, Holy Land."

One oldtimer, leaning against a maple tree, outside, drawled, "There ain't no boat abuildin' round here 'cept the *Nellie Chapin* in Knowles's Yard over ter Addison."

Nobody knew it, but Joshua Adams had already made arrangements for that fine, new bark, and had ordered a second deck to be built to hold the furniture and farming tools that would be needed for the new settlement in Jerusalem.

Today, we assume that this ex-English actor, ex-Mormon preacher practised mass hypnotism, for all at once those usually sensible folks began to dispose of their possessions. They sold their houses and furniture for a song. Cows, pigs and chickens were given away to any who would take care of them. The grass of the parson's lawn was trodden flat by the impatient feet of the faithful coming to hand over their jewelry and family heirlooms and all the cash they could accumulate. Whole families tumbled over their neighbors to sign up for the expedition, although any ten year old schoolboy could have told them that Palestine was no land of milk and honey, as Adams claimed, but an impoverished country swept by sand storms and locusts, a hot, dry, dusty desert where plagues persisted, drinking water was polluted, and strangers were unwelcome. Other such expeditions to the Holy Land had ended in death for the pilgrims at the savage hands of barbaric tribes who swarmed out of the swirling clouds of dust to slay them.

But if anyone showed signs of weakening, Pastor Adams

flew into a rage and reeled off passages from the Good Book to prove that the Israelites and the Saviour were about to return to Jerusalem, and that pacified those pious and simple people.

When he was cornered by a group of harder-headed Yankee business men, he confidentially whispered, "Besides the religious purpose of this expedition, there is also a practical side. Think of the advantage of being on the ground first when thousands of people come back to their homeland! They will need food, clothing, supplies. We will establish stores, schools and banks. You know what it means to get a corner lot on the main street!"

Such palaver didn't fool all of the Yankees. A few level-headed folks tried in every way possible to keep their friends and relatives from embarking on such a hopeless expedition, and when Adams found out about that, he quoted scripture and pounded the pulpit so hard he loosened the nails in it. He stamped on the sagging boards until little clouds of dust rose into the shafts of sunlight, and the windows rattled.

Beads of perspiration streamed down his face as he tore off his collar and tie and flung them to the floor saying sarcastically, "If you need proof that Palestine is a land of milk and honey and opportunity, choose from your number any man to accompany me at my expense to the Holy Land. Let him see with his own eyes and tell you with his own lips."

Before the sun had dropped behind the pine trees, the disciples had chosen a local merchant, Abram K. McKenzie, and shortly thereafter he and Parson Adams sailed from

Jonesport. While they were gone, preparations went ahead for the exodus from Indian River, and when they returned with enthusiastic descriptions of the Promised Land, many Doubting Thomases joined the ranks. But not Mr. McKenzie, who for some reason was quite content to remain in Maine!

Then followed weeks of feverish activity. The six hundred ton three-masted barkentine *Nellie Chapin* was loaded with furniture, food, pine lumber, potatoes, piles of canvas and supplies. Enough lumber was stowed in her hold to build a church, a schoolhouse and twenty dwellings. Enough food and water was taken aboard for two hundred souls, and according to one eye witness, there was plenty of rum for Pastor Adams, who drank heavily all during the voyage.

Adams kept from his followers one fact which might—or might not—have brought them to their senses. He had in his possession a cable from the American consul at Constantinople stating, "THE SULTAN OF TURKEY HAS REFUSED PERMISSION FOR THE ESTABLISHMENT OF YOUR PROPOSED COLONY IN PALESTINE."

Nevertheless, on a sparkling summer day in August, 1866, a long procession wound through the streets of Jonesport, to the vessel tied up at the wharf. Besides the crew in command of Capt. Warren Wass, there were one hundred eighty-six men, women and children, from Addison, Indian River, Jonesport, South Lebanon, Surry and York, Maine, and a few from Rochester, New Hampshire.

Hundreds gathered to watch the departure and say farewell. Old people embraced sons and daughters. Neighbors that had worked side by side throughout a lifetime clasped hands. Brothers and sisters and friends looked for a long time into each other's faces.

"Goodbye . . . . goodbye. God bless you."

The gangplank was hauled aboard and secured. The fore and aft lines were cast off. Then a tug gently moved the *Nellie Chapin* stern first, and soon there was blue water between the barkentine and the tiny, crowded wharf. From the quarter deck, Captain Wass shouted orders to his mates, the Hinckley brothers.

Midship, a little boy and girl stood close together, smelling the pungent tar and rope, hearing the loud, lusty language of the crew, staring up fascinated as the men climbed aloft to loosen the gaskets of the foretopsail, then ranged out on the yard arm. These two children and a few others survived, but most on board that ship were to leave their bones in the sun-baked desert of Jaffa, more than seven thousand miles away.

Now the tug cast off and sails were set. Parson Adams, standing unsteadily on the deck that rose and fell with the gentle swell raised his arms and invoked the Lord's blessing on his victims who knelt before him. Faster and faster the ripples danced from the prow, louder and louder the wind whistled through the shrouds.

Fainter and fainter became the voices on the shore, singing the beloved old hymn, "God Be With You Till We Meet Again."

The passengers spent most of their time in prayer and religious discussion because George Joshua Adams had promised they would meet the Messiah in Palestine and work with Him. Adams had described a lovely, lush country where dates and figs, oranges and olives grew with no care at all.

"Never again," he said, "will you have to shovel snow, or work hard."

Palestine, so Parson Adams said, was a land of love, leisure and luxury. He promised them holy blessings and financial success. In fact, he promised them everything, well backed up by quotations from the Scripture.

The pine-clad shores of Maine had hardly dropped below the horizon before the pilgrims sensed that all was not right with their leader. At the very first prayer meeting they noticed that his usually pale face was flushed, and his usually eloquent voice was thick, and, although the sea was calm, he swayed unsteadily. There were days when he was too drunk to conduct services, but in spite of this shameful performance, the simple-hearted group did not blame nor upbraid their prophet. To them he was a messenger of the Lord, and they were servants to do his bidding. They followed him blindly, for he had cast a spell upon them.

They sang their hymns and gave humble thanks for the fine, fair weather and the quick passage to Gibraltar which rose one morning like a loaf of New England brown bread, out of the pink and purple dawn. Children and grown-ups alike stared wide-eyed and excited at the white stucco houses on the sharp gray slopes of the shore. A bronze-faced fisherman looked at the unfamiliar lateen sails and allowed as how you "couldn't ketch lobsters or mackerel in them flimsy things."

A couple, long past middle age, stood staring at the noble

rock. "Who'd ever thought we'd be seeing Gibraltar? But 'tain't half so purty as Kineo or Katahdin."

If the approach to Jaffa was disappointing, nobody said so. It was the Promised Land, and beyond those cactus-covered piles of rock that looked so dry and dreary and doleful in the blazing sun, there must be fertile fields and valleys. Parson Adams had said so.

The lookout, high on the foremast, was the first to sense danger. His sharp eyes and keen nose caught the drifting cloud of dust and the stench that rolled out from shore. He looked down onto the little band of pilgrims gathered on deck for final prayers and sadly realized that only evil would come out of that sun-baked land of lice and locusts. What a pity they could not have known this, and turned back while there was still time!

Instead, in the brief cool hour before sunrise, they scrambled into boats to row ashore, the women and children then being carried through the shallow water "pig-a-back" clinging to the filthy rags of Arab beggars who stuck out grimy palms crying, "Backsheesh, backsheesh!" They were horrible looking, and the children were afraid.

It was several days before the furniture, lumber and Maine potatoes were ferried ashore. Meantime the pilgrims lived in tents set up in an orange grove, the only shelter anywhere from the burning, blistering sun. (Years later, a man, who was a child then, remembered the sweet, juicy oranges as the only pleasant thing in Palestine.)

When all the water they had brought from Maine was gone, they lowered buckets into the evil-smelling wells nearby. Their physician, Dr. Calvin Higgins, a graduate of Dartmouth Medical School, warned that every drop of water must be boiled before they drank it. He would not even let them bathe their swollen eyes and sun-baked faces for fear of infection.

There were sudden, extreme changes of temperature. All day the sun beat down on the hard-packed sand, but at night it was cold. There were swarms of flies, and bugs crawled over everybody and everything. Some folks caught fever and died immediately, and on the plain where Joshua commanded the sun to stand still, were buried with only a crude wooden cross to mark their graves.

Somehow the men managed to build a little village, a church, a school, and some homes, and as late as World War II, some of those buildings were standing, one of them with a white picket fence built by a Maine carpenter!

What must have been the feelings of those Yankees, who found to their amazement that the Promised Land was as primitive as in the days of Abraham? There wasn't a single wheeled vehicle to be seen; the wells from which water was drawn in goat skins were old as history, and among the pock-marked beggars who took water from them, there were many lepers. The very air seemed full of maggots and fleas.

Food became scarce and the all but starving pilgrims from Jonesport were reduced to bread, molasses and a few oranges. They had planted potatoes, and Arthur Rogers, who was eight years old at the time, remembered the ground was so hard they had to dig them out with a pickax, worthless little spuds no bigger than walnuts. Mr. Rogers lived to be almost ninety, and after he returned to his home in

Maine, he often talked about the pilgrimage to his daughter Mrs. Oscar H. Dunbar of Machias. He well remembered how one brother died of smallpox, and another was born as if to take his place.

"All through the hardship and sorrow," Mr. Rogers said, "Pastor Adams moved serenely, advising those who had fever to 'Drink rum, my brother, and abide in the Lord.'" Always, Adams had a verse of Scripture on his tongue, when the bottle was not there.

Mr. Rogers remembered that the milk was always full of hairs from the goatskin bags, and that they had to melt and strain the butter three or four times to get rid of the bugs, and that there were the red and green growths that formed in it.

Another survivor of the Palestine pilgrimage was Mrs. Frances M. Paul of West Haven, Connecticut. She, and her mother and father and brother Eli and sister Sophia had hardly got settled in their new house at Jaffa when all of them except little Frances were struck down with fever. As she sat by her mother's bedside in the stifling heat, trying to brush away the flies, her mother smiled and said, "Don't mind me, dear, look after the others. And be a good girl."

She closed her weary eyes, and did not speak again. Frances buried her mother with her own hands, behind the new house, and went back to do what she could for her father and brother and sister. Dr. Higgins told her, "There is no hope for any of them."

The next day, her father was burning with fever. "Go to the well, Frances," he moaned, "and get me some water.

I am dying of thirst! And don't boil it, I want some cold water; I want some real water such as we had at home!"

Frances ran to the well, hauled up a pail of brackish water and placed a dipperful in his shaking hands.

"Drink all you want, Father," she said, holding back the tears. "It will make you strong and well." And he gulped down every bit of the germ laden water.

The hot afternoon dragged on. While her father slept, Frances sat by the window and fanned away the flies. It was very, very still. She thought of her old home in Indian River, of the big lilac bush that stood beside the barn, and the sweet smelling haymow where she played on rainy days. She remembered how they used to go after wild strawberries and come home with stained faces and fingers, and a full dish, and her mother would be waiting with new hot biscuits and a pitcher of cream.

She looked down at the ugly mound of earth in the yard. Not even a blade of green grass on her mother's grave!

Then her father called and she went to him. His voice was weak. "Frances," he said, "prop me up so I can see the sun go down. I want to die looking toward Maine."

He turned his tired face toward the window. Above the Mediterranean, the sun was dropping into a purple bank of heavy clouds, their edges rimmed with gold. The harbor was hot and dazzling. She raised the curtain a little and said, "The sun's going down fast, Father. It will be cooler pretty soon."

Suddenly he cried out. "Look, Daughter! Look!"

Frances saw a ship gliding smoothly into the calm, silvery

harbor of Jaffa, and as it turned, she caught sight of the flag hanging limp at the stern.

"It's an American gunboat, Frances! The Stars and Stripes! Get me down to the shore quickly! Get me down there!"

With the help of some natives, Frances managed to get her ailing father down to the water's edge and onto a raft. She and an Arab boy, with long sticks for oars, paddled out to the gunboat.

"We are Americans," she called, looking up at the men lining the rail of the vessel. "My father is dying. Please help us."

The sailors took them aboard the warship, and then lowered a boat and went after her brother and sister. They cared for them all, and carried them from Palestine to Alexandria, where later they embarked for home. Frances' father recovered, and lived to be a hale old man who boasted about his narrow escape from death.

"We left everything we had," Mrs. Paul said afterward. "All our clothes and dishes and furniture, and poor dear mother in her lonely grave."

A few others deserted the colony, and forty or so more were taken on board the cruise ship *Quaker City*. Among the passengers on the *Quaker City* was Mark Twain who described his long trip in *Innocents Abroad*. Of the "Jaffa Colonists" he wrote:

"At Jaffa we had taken on board some forty members of a very celebrated community. They were male and female; babies, young boys and young girls; young married people, and some who had passed a shade beyond the prime of life. We left in Jaffa Mr. Adams, his wife, and fifteen unfortunates who not only had no money, but did not know where to turn or whither to go. Such was the statement made to us. Our forty were miserable enough in the first place, and they lay about the decks sea-sick all the voyage, which about completed their misery, I take it. However, one or two young men remained upright, and by constant persecution we wormed out of them some little information. They gave it reluctantly and in a very fragmentary condition, for, having been shamefully humbugged by their prophet, they felt humiliated and unhappy. In such circumstances people do not like to talk.

"The colony was a complete fiasco. I have already said that such as could get away did so, from time to time. The prophet Adams—once an actor, then several other things, afterward a Mormon and a missionary, always an adventurer—remains at Jaffa with his handful of sorrowful subjects. The forty we brought away with us were chiefly destitute, though not all of them. They wished to get to Egypt. What might become of them then they did not know and probably did not care—anything to get away from hated Jaffa. They had little to hope for. . . .

"Thus circumstanced, they landed at Alexandria from our ship. One of our passengers, Mr. Moses S. Beach, of the New York *Sun*, inquired of the Consul-general what it would cost to send these people to their home in Maine, and he said fifteen hundred dollars in gold would do it. Mr. Beach gave his cheque for the money, and so the troubles of the Jaffa colonists were at an end."

But this last was hardly true. Out of the one hundred

eighty-six pilgrims, perhaps sixty returned to America, most of them without a possession in the world. Few of them cared to face the scorn of their old friends in Maine, and they scattered over the country to make new homes among strangers.

Human Hibernation

EVERYBODY HAS HEARD about "dead" birds picked up after a blizzard and revived in a warm room, and fishermen by the hundred recall occasions when a frozen-solid pail of pickerel was melted, and the fish started swimming; and there have been several cases where humans revived, and survived, after being pronounced dead by freezing.

These occurrences have a certain aura about them—is it supernatural? miraculous?—which makes them always fascinating. When a Russian scientist announced a few years ago that he had found fungi, bacteria and moulds buried for centuries in the vast Siberian deep-freeze, and had successfully brought them back to life, newspapers all over the world gave his discovery a big play. Readers of all ages, in all walks of life, everywhere, saw these articles and pondered over them.

Up in the Green Mountain State of Vermont, Elbert S.

Stevens of Bridgewater Corners, when he read these reports, puffed on his pipe and drawled, "I guess them Rooshians never heard 'bout freezing the old folks up back of Montpelier. When Marm told us that story of a winter's night, us kids got goose-pimples."

The boys at the General Store kicked the spittoon out of the way and moved in close. "Tell us abaout it, Elbert."

Mr. Stevens hitched his thumbs comfortably under his galluses. "Seems there was a famine round here, and to save grub and firewood, some of the old folks who couldn't work for their vittles was given a good big supper and put outdoors to FREEZE! By midnight they was stiff as stove-pokers. Next morning they was piled in a box, covered with straw and sledded out under a big ledge. There they stayed, under them snow-drifts, all winter!

"Come spring, they was dug out and put in warm water. Soon's any of 'em showed signs of coming to, they give him a slug of brandy, wrapped him in blankets and took him home. After a few good feeds they was fit as fiddles and them that was able set to work planting corn."

Mr. Stevens pulled at the tarnished ends of his handlebar mustache and added, "It was all printed in the paper and I have the clipping Marm pasted in her scrapbook. I've read it hundreds of times."

The General Store Boys shook their heads, some sidewise, some up and down, and without much conviction either way. Not long afterward, the curious tale came to the ears of a staff reporter of the Rutland *Herald*. Hunting up the aged Mr. Stevens, he borrowed the old scrapbook, and on

May 24, 1939, the whole eerie yarn came out in his paper. The following is a verbatim copy of the yellowed clipping.

"A Strange Tale"
By A. M.

"I am an old man now, and have seen some strange sights in the course of a roving life in foreign lands as well as in this country, but none so strange as one I found recorded in an old diary, kept by my Uncle William, that came into my possession a few years ago, at his decease. The events described took place in a mountain town some twenty miles from Montpelier, the Capital of Vermont. I have been to the place on the mountain, and seen the old log-house where the events I found recorded in the diary took place, and seen and talked with an old man who vouched for the truth of the story, and that his father was one of the parties operated on. The account runs in this wise:

" '*January* 7.–I went on the mountain today, and witnessed what to me was a horrible sight. It seems that the dwellers there, who are unable, either from age or other reasons, to contribute to the support of their families, are disposed of in the winter months in a manner that will shock the one who reads this diary, unless that person lives in that vicinity. I will describe what I saw. Six persons, four men and two women, one of the men a cripple about 30 years old, the other five past the age of usefulness, lay on the earthy floor of the cabin drugged into insensibility, while members of their families were gathered about them in apparent indifference. In a short time the unconscious bodies were inspected by one man who said, "They are ready." They were then stripped of all their clothing, except a single garment. Then the bodies were carried outside, and laid on logs exposed to the bitter cold mountain air, the operation having been delayed several days for suitable weather.

" 'It was night when the bodies were carried out, and the full moon, occasionally obscured by flying clouds, shone on their upturned ghastly faces, and a horrible fascination kept me by the bodies as long as I could endure the severe cold. Soon the noses, ears and fingers began to turn white, then the limbs and face assumed a tallowy look. I could stand the cold no longer, and went inside, where I found the friends in cheerful conversation.

" 'In about an hour I went out and looked at the bodies: they were fast freezing. Again I went inside, where the men were smoking their clay pipes, but silence had fallen on them; perhaps they were thinking of the time when their turn would come to be cared for in the same way. One by one they at last lay down on the floor, and went to sleep. It seemed a horrible nightmare to me, and I could not think of sleep. I could not shut out the sight of those freezing bodies outside, neither could I bear to be in darkness, but I piled on the wood in the cavernous fireplace, and, seated on a shingle block, passed the dreary night, terror-stricken by the horrible sights I had witnessed.

" '*January 8.*–Day came at length, but did not dissipate the terror that filled me. The frozen bodies became visible, white as the snow that lay in huge drifts about them. The women gathered about the fire, and soon commenced preparing breakfast. The men awoke, and, conversation again commencing, affairs assumed a more cheerful aspect. After breakfast the men lighted their pipes, and some of them took a yoke of oxen and went off toward the forest, while others proceeded to nail together boards, making a box about ten feet long and half as high and wide. When this was completed they placed about two feet of straw in the bottom; then they laid three of the frozen bodies on the straw. Then the faces and upper part of the bodies were covered with a cloth, then more straw was put in the box, and the other three bodies placed on top and covered the same as the first ones, with cloth and straw. Boards were then firmly nailed on the top, to protect the bodies from being injured by carnivorous animals that make their home on these mountains.

" 'By this time the men who went off with the ox-team returned with a huge load of spruce and hemlock boughs, which they unloaded at the foot of a steep ledge, came to the house and loaded the box containing the bodies on the sled, and drew it to the foot of the ledge, near the load of boughs. These were soon piled on and around the box, and it was left to be covered up with snow, which I was told would lie in drifts twenty feet deep over this rude tomb. "We shall want our men to plant our corn next spring," said a youngish looking woman, the wife of one of the frozen men, "and if you want to see them resuscitated, you come here about the 10th of next May."

" 'With this agreement, I left the mountaineers, both the living and the frozen, to their fate and I returned to my home in Boston where it was weeks before I was fairly myself, as my thoughts would return to that mountain with its awful sepulchre.' Turning the leaves of the diary, the old man recounts, the following entry was found:

"'*May 10.*—I arrived here at 10 A. M., after riding about four hours over muddy, unsettled roads. The weather is warm and pleasant, most of the snow is gone, except here and there drifts in the fence corners and hollows, but nature is not yet dressed in green. I found the same parties here that I left last January, ready to disinter the bodies of their friends. I had no expectation of finding any life there, but a feeling that I could not resist impelled me to come and see. We repaired at once to the well remembered spot, at the ledge. The snow had melted from the top of the brush, but still lay deep around the bottom of the pile. The men commenced work at once, some shoveling away the snow, and others tearing away the brush. Soon the box was visible. The cover was taken off, the layers of straw removed, and the bodies, frozen and apparently lifeless, lifted out and laid on the snow. Large troughs made out of hemlock logs were placed nearby, filled with tepid water, into which the bodies were separately placed, with the head slightly raised. Boiling water was then poured into the trough from kettles hung on poles over fires near by, until the water in the trough was as hot as I could hold my hand in. Hemlock boughs had been put in the boiling water in such quantities that they had given the water the color of wine. After lying in this bath about an hour, color began to return to the bodies, when all hands began rubbing and chafing them. This continued about another hour, when a slight twitching of the muscles of the face and limbs, followed by audible gasps, showed that life was not quenched, and that vitality was returning. Spirits were then given in small quantities, and allowed to trickle down their throats. Soon they could swallow, and more was given them, when their eyes opened, and they began to talk, and finally sat up in their bathtubs. They were then taken out and assisted to the house, where after a hearty dinner they seemed as well as ever, and in nowise injured, but rather refreshed, by their long sleep of four months.' Truly, truth is stranger than fiction."

Four days later, on May 28, 1939, the Boston Sunday *Globe* carried this headline: "HUMAN HIBERNATION IN VERMONT CENTURY AGO."

"Montpelier, Vt. May 27–Recent experiments with freezing of humans so that all bodily functions were suspended for hours, described at the sessions of the American Medical Association in St. Louis, were merely the beginning of possibilities in this direction, according to goings-on in a tiny village near here nearly a century ago.

"A recent issue of the Rutland *Herald* carried a reprint of a clipping taken from an old scrapbook belonging to Elbert S. Stevens of Bridgewater Corners in which he described the strange adventures of a traveler in Vermont in the 90's." Then followed the reprint, "A Strange Tale, by A. M."

Yankee magazine printed the grisly tale in 1940 and it created so much speculation, from far-afield points, that Publisher Robb Sagendorph included the story of "Frozen Death" in the 1943 edition of the famous *Old Farmer's Almanac.*

B. A. Botkin borrowed the chiller from the *Almanac* for his *A Treasury of New England Folklore.*

The story was now well on its way to becoming a classic, and all over the country youngsters shuddered delightfully while old and feeble folks were understandably repelled.

Charles Edward Crane, distinguished Vermont author and historian, gave the story a place in his book, *Winter in Vermont* and to answer innumerable questions, he broadcast, not once but several times, over Montpelier's radio station. I also broadcast the story.

Anxious to see the clipping and interview Mr. Stevens, and photograph them both before anything happened to them, I had driven to Vermont and found the old-timer in his accustomed corner of the general store. He said if I didn't mind walking down the "rudd" a piece, I could see the scrapbook.

"Don't mind the mess," he puffed, leading me up a rickety flight of stairs on the outside of a rambling, unpainted two-story structure. "Since my last wife died, I've kinda let things go."

The living room was a clutter of old clothes, dishes and pile upon pile of books, papers and magazines. On a shelf, two carved female faces stared woodenly from under the brims of old-fashioned headgear. "My late wives," Elbert explained. "Dead and gone a long time. I carved 'em out of a chunk of pine. Keeps me from being lonesome."

Reaching into a closet, he held up a pig's head, also whittled from wood. "*He* was a good pal too."

While I returned the stares of the wooden wives and the pig, Mr. Stevens did considerable rummaging, finally handing me the scrapbook—a bulky, heavy, leather-bound volume entitled: *Messages of the President of the United*

States to the Two Houses of Congress at the Commencement of the Thirty-Seventh Congress. 1862. Vol. I.

Originally this voluminous report had contained 910 pages, but Mother Stevens had clipped a few pages here and there to allow room for the births, marriages, deaths, recipes, poems and local doings which had taken her fancy. On page 62 was "A Strange Tale, by A. M." but there was nothing to show when it had been published, nor by what newspaper. After a cursory examination of the dusty book, I made a few photographs and then turned my attention to Elbert Stevens.

"Do you believe that story?"

He exploded. "Course I do! My mother told me about freezing them old people!"

Back in Boston I prepared my radio script, never dreaming that this tale of "Frozen Death" would arouse so much interest, indignation and speculation. Immediately following the broadcast we were flooded with phone calls and letters.

"Missed your hibernation story; please repeat it."

"Don't tell me you fell for such a hoax."

"Who was Uncle William and where is his diary?"

The prize and not-so-serious letter came from a listener up in Cal Coolidge's country. "After reading how the Washington experts (?) got the farmers to plow under their crops, kill their hogs, and dump thousands of bushels of potatoes to rot, I'm worrying for fear they'll start freezing us old folks to conserve food and fuel." It was signed, "Lifelong Republican."

Concurrently, as this story rolled along, gathering momentum, newspapers and magazines printed other stories of *FREEZING*, and in several instances the Vermont episode was quoted as fact.

Dr. Gregory Pincus of Clark University described an experiment in which the male cells of a man, a bull, and frogs were plunged into liquid nitrogen, frozen solid, and later thawed gradually, and to everyone's astonishment 50 per cent of the cells were alive.

A new treatment for cancer was being tried. An item from Springfield, Illinois, stated: "A man was restored to life after having been frozen in an unconscious sleep for five days and nights in an amazing experiment to rid his body of deadly cancer." The patient was placed in a tub and packed with ice until his body temperature was reduced to 84 degrees. Whether or not the cancer was cured, a serious heart condition apparently was, and doctors suggested that hibernation might be employed in the treatment of cardiac patients. Anyway, the man awoke from his iced sleep smiling and feeling fine.

Bernarr MacFadden in *Physical Culture* helped matters along by writing that "frozen sleep" treatment for cancer was not really so revolutionary—six persons had once been frozen for the winter up near Montpelier, Vermont. This was quite in accord with a long-held theory of his, that human bodies could be frozen and brought back to life in the same manner as certain animals.

Describing the use of low temperature, which numbs the nerve ends, as a local anaesthetic, more than one medical man anticipated a time when the entire body might be frozen and revived "as was done in Vermont many years ago." Dr. Fay of Temple University, who performed early cold-therapy experiments with cancer patients, was quoted as saying he accepted the story as fact.

I, myself, confronted a famous New York diagnostician, and asked him point blank if he thought the scrapbook story was possible. He was a long time answering. "While I doubt if any such event ever took place as described in this story, so many remarkable experiments have been conducted along this line that I hesitate to say it is impossible."

Scientific progress was all around me, and *FREEZING* seemed to be in the very air. By this time, and not alone by any means, I began to wonder if "A Strange Tale, by A. M." could be true!

Among the many with whom I discussed this mystery was Roland Wells Robbins, a local archeologist with a penchant for digging up facts. Mr. Robbins had just settled a fifty-year-old controversy concerning the exact location of the hut in which Thoreau lived and wrote at Walden Pond. For years visitors had been piling stones on a cairn in Concord, Massachusetts, believing it was the site of Thoreau's cabin. Robbins spent two years reading, probing, measuring and digging until he unearthed the actual foundation of the cabin; this was fascinating business for Robbins.

After that he turned to pre-restoration archeological work at the site of the First Iron Works, at Saugus, Massachusetts, for the American Iron and Steel Institute. I was interviewing him on location when suddenly he changed the subject.

"That story about freezing old folks up in Vermont. . . ." he began.

"Yes," I said, "that is a puzzler. I've never known a story to get such a hold on people."

"I'm going up to Vermont and solve that mystery if it takes ten years. Will you tell me all you know about it?"

I hesitated. I was fond of the tall tale and it had done well for me as it had for quite a few others, and I rather disliked having it debunked. But of course I was anxious to learn who had written the story originally, what paper had printed it, and what had inspired the strange tale.

Robbins began, as I had ten years before, with a trip to Bridgewater Corners, but Elbert Stevens, now over eighty, wasn't living there any more. "You'll find Elbert," drawled one of his neighbors, "over ter Woodstock in the County Jail. But 'tain't as bad as it sounds; he's jest boarding there for the winter."

By the time Robbins reached Woodstock, Elbert had moved to a better boarding place, up in Rutland. Bundling the old fellow into his car, Robbins drove over slippery, snowy roads to the cold, empty house in Bridgewater Corners. Elbert produced the scrapbook, and Robbins took it to his hotel.

On the fly-leaf was written "Hannah F. Stevens, Bridgewater, Vermont, July 24th, 1895." But the earliest clipping was dated 1879, so Robbins concluded that the article about Frozen Death had been clipped from some local newspaper between those dates. But which newspaper?

Examining the clipping carefully, he noted that a thin black line ran down the left side of the column but not down the right, indicating that it had appeared on the right hand side of a page. A decorative space line below the story showed that it didn't quite fill the column, and, by measuring, Robbins found that the newspaper had used wider and longer columns than most papers of those days.

His next step was to visit the State Library at Montpelier where he examined files of old newspapers. Only one used the same width of column—the Montpelier *Argus & Patriot.* So far, so good, but as the task of going through bound volumes of the *Argus* for sixteen years seemed hopeless, he "split the difference" between 1879 and 1895, and began with the file for 1886. No luck. He examined the file for 1885. Nothing there.

He had reached the last few pages of the 1887 file when his heart leaped! "A Strange Tale, by A. M." had first been printed on Wednesday, December 21, 1887!

Above the title was the line (which had been snipped off the clipping in the Stevens scrapbook), "Written for the *Argus & Patriot.*" Evidently, then, "A. M." was a regular contributor, and it should be easy, Robbins figured, to find other stories bearing that by-line. But a search of the entire newspaper files for 1887 and 1888 proved fruitless. The nearest he came to it was one poem by "A. H. Mills of Middlebury."

Stranger still, he found no reference to the freezing episode in later editions. Had the story excited no interest, no curiosity, in that generation?

Baffled, but unwilling to give up his research, Mr. Robbins toured the towns within a twenty-five miles radius of Montpelier, where the freezings were said to have taken place. Almost everyone knew the story, but no one could add anything new.

Hoping someone would yet come forward with the information he wanted, Robbins prepared a lengthy article which was published in the 1949 winter edition of *Vermont Life*, the official publication of the State of Vermont. The following (spring 1950) issue said editorially, "The article on 'Human Hibernation' evoked an avalanche of letters, phone calls and newspaper comment. One columnist suggests that 'A. M.' might have been some member of the Atkins family, who owned and published the *Argus & Patriot* in 1887. Several members of that family have initials 'M. A.' which might simply be reversed."

But Robbins had already interviewed Miss Elaine Atkins, editor and publisher of the Montpelier *Argus* (now a daily) and reached another dead end. Old office records had been destroyed by flood or by fire; there was nothing left to identify old-time contributors.

Among the letters which Robbins received, one from Florida seemed promising. Mrs. Mabel E. Hynes wrote, "The A. M. you are looking for was my grandfather, Allen Morse." Robbins would have liked to have jumped a plane that very day, but his duties at the Iron Works kept him in Saugus, and impatiently he sweated it out until Mrs. Hynes returned to her home in Massachusetts where he could talk to her.

This is what he learned: Allen Morse was born in Woodbury, Vermont, on December 21, 1835. The family moved to Calais, Vermont, in 1840, and there he lived most of his life. He had four children, three girls and one boy. The eldest girl, Alice May Morse (Mrs. Hynes' mother), secured her first employment in the *Argus & Patriot* office in Montpelier and "took board and room" with the publisher, Hiram Atkins.

Like most Vermonters, Allen Morse devoted much of his time to farming, but he was also of a literary bent and frequently wrote pieces for the *New England Homestead* and for *Farm & Fireside*. That he was progressive and thrifty is shown by his purchasing the first parlor organ and the first sewing machine in that section of Vermont. The organ was used freely for Sunday night gatherings, but neighbors were charged by the yard when they borrowed the sewing machine.

Allen Morse was noted as story teller, and no family reunion or Christmas party went by that he wasn't called upon to spin a few yarns. Benjamin Morse, his cousin, was runner-up, and considerable rivalry existed between A. M. and B. M. to see who could tell the tallest tale.

Benjamin's favorite spell-binder concerned a grave which burst into flame, and not to be outdone, Allen Morse concocted his freezing story, using familiar local spots to make it sound real. The cabin where the bodies were prepared was an old deserted log house near the Morse farm, and the ledge where they lay under the snow was Eagle Ledge, on the road between Calais and East Elmore. And incidentally, the snow has been known to drift to a depth of twenty feet and more at that particular place.

The "Uncle William," mentioned was a brother-in-law, William Noyes.

Mrs. Hynes explained, "My mother left the *Argus & Patriot* after she married and moved to Connecticut, but she frequently came back to Vermont for short visits.

Around the middle of December, 1887, she called on her former employer, Hiram Atkins, and suggested he print her father's favorite story on his birthday."

Editor Atkins read over the handwritten pages about the alleged freezings and smiled. "I'll print it if you'll set it." So, borrowing an apron and a composing stick, Allen Morse's daughter set the type from which "A Strange Tale, by A. M." was printed on her father's fifty-second birthday, December 21, 1887.

Over in Bridgewater, Mrs. Hannah Stevens, interested by the story, cut it out and pasted it into her scrapbook, never dreaming that half a century later, authors, editors, newspaper reporters and photographers would be pestering her son Elbert for just a peek at the old clipping. And how surprised "A. M." would have been to read in all the books and papers and magazines this tall tale he had invented in his effort to tell a bigger lie than his cousin!

In spite of the fact that this famous Vermont legend has been debunked, it will still be told when Yankee families gather round their firesides on future winter nights. Fiction though it was, it caught the public's interest, and fooled not a few. And, considering what has been accomplished since that time with low-temperature treatments in medical research, who can say that it was not prophetic?

The Dugway

In the course of my radio broadcasts, several listeners asked if I would tell about the digging of the Dugway at Vergennes, Vermont, during the war of 1812.

You won't find much about this incident in history books, but if you care to get a boat and drift slowly down Otter Creek, from Vergennes to where the stream empties into Lake Champlain, you can still find traces of that historic ditch, and in the main square at Vergennes there is a fine monument to Commodore Thomas Macdonough, who engineered the Dugway, and because of it, got his flatboats and fleet out of Otter Creek and onto Lake Champlain.

Tom Macdonough enlisted in the American navy—such as it was—when he was seventeen, and after the bombardment of Tripoli he was promoted to Lieutenant. When the United States declared war against Great Britain in 1812, Tom, then only twenty-nine, was ordered to Lake Champlain to guard the northern gateway between the United States and Canada.

To appreciate what he was up against, we must not only consider conditions here at home, but take a good look at what England had up her sleeve. With her overwhelming naval power, Great Britain, by 1814, had swept the seas clean of American commerce. All of our harbors were closed, our warships were blockaded in their ports, and industry was paralyzed. All that remained for the complete subjugation of this new Yankee republic was an English army on American soil. So, as soon as the British had slapped down Napoleon and taken Paris, the "Invincibles" were sent across the Atlantic to land in Chesapeake Bay and in Canada.

The plan was obvious. One British army would attack the national capital at Washington, then move north, while the other would sail down Lake Champlain to invade Vermont and New York. With the most ships, the biggest guns, an unlimited amount of ammunition and veteran troops fresh from a smashing victory over Napoleon—how could they lose?

Now let's see what we had to fight the British with in this war that commenced in June, 1812.

Our army at that time consisted of twenty-one regiments (one thousand men to a regiment). This was increased on paper to fifty-eight regiments, but it is doubtful if one sixth of that number were ever recruited, and they were mostly scattered at Indian outposts in the middle west. It should be mentioned here that this homespun army of untrained, peace-loving Yankees, possessing only makeshift ordnance, would have to face the toughest gangs of well-armed "gorillas" ever turned loose on civilized communities. That isn't my opinion, but the word of their own commander, Lord Wellington. He had led them to victory over the Emperor of France, but he could not control or restrain them. They had burned and raped and killed in terrifying onslaughts as they advanced through Europe. These, then, were the kind of troops being rushed across the sea to attack Washington in the south and the "Gateway of the North" at Lake Champlain.

Macdonough, hearing that some enemy scout ships were at the upper end of Lake Champlain, dispatched his "fleet" to attack them. His fleet consisted of two small sloops of war, the *Growler* and the *Eagle;* the British ships sailed away from them, up the Sorel River—the all-too-eager Yankees followed right into a trap and were captured. Macdonough didn't have any navy, and all the time the British were landing additional troops for smash attacks on Saratoga and Plattsburg. The southern force had already landed in Chesapeake Bay, captured Washington, burned the Capitol.

It was mighty lucky for us that Capt. Thomas Macdonough was in charge of affairs at Lake Champlain in such a critical situation. He proved to be wise, sagacious, and wholly without fear of superior numbers.

Instead of building his new fleet on the shores of Lake Champlain, Macdonough went inland some seven miles up Otter Creek, to Vergennes, where there was an iron foundry, a rolling mill, and several good-sized saw mills. There, too, he found just the kind of Yankee craftsmen he needed, and without waiting for word from Washington,

Macdonough seized a merchant ship, converted her into a war vessel and renamed her the *Preble*. Then he found an old tub which he partially rebuilt, installed some cannon, and christened *Ticonderoga*. Then he laid the keel of a full rigged ship, also to be fully armed, which he christened *Saratoga*.

While the shipbuilders were sweating day and night to complete these three war vessels, forge and foundry were turning out cannon and shot like nobody's business.

In Vergennes there lived a first-class carpenter named John Roberts. Macdonough hunted him up and asked, "Can you build some flat-bottomed boats capable of carrying a mortar, mast and sail, and a company of men?"

Roberts said he could, and they went to work, and in the incredible short space of forty days, Thomas Macdonough had a whole new fleet to fight with.

He was then just thirty years old!

Tom had barely got his little fleet finished when winter set in, the creek froze over, and with no chance of getting down the stream into the lake, he drilled his men, tested his guns and made plans. With the coming of spring, he was ready to slip down the creek the day the ice melted. But one of his scouts brought word that three big British ships, moving through the ice cakes, had come down lake from Canada and had anchored off the mouth of the Otter River, thus blockading him. Temporarily, he postponed his sailing—not because he did not dare to face the enemy, but because he wanted to reach the scene of battle intact.

Macdonough knew he could not afford to lose a single

man or ship, the odds were that great; so he waited, but he did get awfully impatient.

One day he called his officers together and said, "I have just received word that Prevost is planning to take Plattsburg, so I guess we will have to make a running fight for it, dangerous though it is."

The younger officers cheered, but the more experienced men shook their heads. "We won't have a chance, Sir; they'll blow us right out of the water."

At that moment, a tousle haired lad of seventeen stepped up and drawled, "I know how you can get inter the lake if you're willing to try sompin . . . ."

"You do? HOW?"

The youth scratched his head and said slowly, "Waal, I've spent a lot of time on the crick, fishin' and so forth, and I know where there's a shaller place what makes in back of the mouth of the crick, and I was just thinking . . . ."

"Yes! Yes, Boy! Go on!"

"Waal, I was thinking if you had enough men with picks and shovels, you could dig through that shaller place some night and float all them barges right out inter the bay."

"In one night, Son?"

"Sure! You could dig ALMOST all the way, then bring the boats down in the dark and bust through in no time. I betcha you could. 'Taint very fur, honest."

The older officers smiled and turned away, but Macdonough motioned the boy to follow him. An hour later they were in a bateau, cautiously rowing down Otter Creek.

They had reached the last bend in the stream, about a

third of a mile from Lake Champlain, when the boy pointed. "There's the place. Come on ashore; I'll show yer."

Sure enough, after they had scrambled through alders, swamp maples and cattails, and gained the wooded crest of a small rise, they could see through the trees, the wind whipped waters of Lake Champlain.

Macdonough said under his breath, "Well, I'll be damned! Not more than one hundred sixty-five yards! You know, Son, I think we can do it!"

His staff, back at the shipyard, thought otherwise; one of the grizzled old workers said sarcastically, "I don't spose them Britishers are going to hear us achoppin' and adiggin'?"

"Not if we work quietly, and with a northwest wind."

"But, surely, Sir, you can't be serious about digging a ditch through this swamp, big enough for the *Saratoga?*"

"Of course not," Macdonough laughed. "That's not the idea." And, picking up a stick, he drew a diagram in the wet sand. "We'll start digging under cover of darkness of course, several rods back from the bay, and let water in. Then, we'll pole the galleys down, and at the last moment, we can break through into the lake.

"I'll arrange for Lieutenant Cassin to fire a signal shot from the fort farther down the shore, the moment he sees us emerge, and I'll wager anything you want to that when those Britishers see the galleys coming into the lake from out of the bushes, they'll be too surprised to notice the bigger ships coming down the main creek."

A few of the officers still protested vigorously against

this daring trick, but all of the younger men were eager to try anything, rather than stay bottled up at Vergennes.

Macdonough waited for a wild windy night, and when low black clouds swept in, bringing sheets of rain, he dispatched boatload after boatload of wood choppers and bush pullers down the creek. They were followed by an army of diggers, Macdonough leading them in their difficult, muddy task. Not a single light was used, and many of the men were up to their armpits in the muck and tangle of swamp roots. At the end of ten days (or nights) the main part of the ditch was finished and filled with water deep enough to float the flatboats! It was tough work pushing, pulling and polling the heavy barges through the bushes, but every man did his damndest, and when all the barges were down stream and in position, the weary, mud-soaked workers sprawled on the decks for a well-earned rest.

Macdonough had thoughtfully posted sentries, mostly Indian scouts, so no British spy might get close enough to see what was going on, and the captains of the bigger ships, still up the creek at Vergennes, were ordered to be ready for a quick dash down stream—at the sound of the cannons from the fort.

Then came a day which presaged one of those thunderstorms for which that region is famous. Masses of thunderheads towered in the sky, an unnatural stillness, not a breath of wind. By late afternoon, black clouds rolled in to bring darkness early, and as soon as it was totally dark, and raining hard, the diggers broke from cover and went to work. At the end of four hours, they had broken through the last barrier of brush, roots and sand, and the first of the galleys sailed into Lake Champlain.

Back a few miles below Vergennes Macdonough spoke to the captains of the *Preble*, *Saratoga* and *Ticonderoga*. "It will be daylight in three hours. So get down stream as far as you can while it is still dark. Keep close to shore at all times. When you hear the cannon, head for the lake at full speed. Keep your guns loaded, and join me in battle if it comes to that. Be of good cheer, Men, and God bless each one of you!"

The stars were still winking through wisps of fog when Macdonough boarded the *Saratoga* and gave orders to cast off. In that pre-dawn darkness, the other ships followed silently, hugging the shore and drifting like ghosts with the sluggish current of Otter Creek. As they reached the river's mouth, darkness gave way to grayness, and to Macdonough's relief, he saw the whole lake was covered with a low-lying blanket of fog. There was no sight or sound of the flatboats hidden along the shore at his right, but out ahead, at the left, in deep water, were the enemy ships, their broad hulls obscured by the fog, only their topmasts showing in the thinning mist.

A tiny breeze ruffled the mirror-like lake, and the British ships could now be seen more distinctly, their bright work sparkling in the rays of the rising sun. Time ticked away; the Yankees itched to get into action.

Suddenly a loud boom broke the morning stillness and went reverberating across the peaceful water! Captain Cassin had seen the first of the flatboats emerge from the shore, and had fired his signal shot from the fort.

As his second signal boomed out, the American ships sprang to life. Yards rattled and blocks creaked (in spite of their many greasings), gunners sprang to their posts, and now, their sails bellying in the faint breeze, the three ships slipped from where they had been hiding, and moved into Lake Champlain.

At the same time, the fully-armed flat-bottomed galleys emerged from the Dugway.

Roused from their slumbers by the unexpected cannon shots, the Britishers stumbled on deck, to perceive, through the drifting fog, what appeared to be TWO fleets, bearing down upon them.

Bugles sounded, chains rattled, oars splashed. Anchors came up, sails were shaken out, and in a matter of minutes, the big British ships were under way. Macdonough crowded on all the canvas he had, but the breeze fushed out, and the bigger and faster enemy ships, farther out in the lake, moved quickly ahead of him, soon to vanish into the mist headed for the upper part of Lake Champlain and Canada. Macdonough did not pursue them at this time. It was enough of a victory for him that, by digging the Dugway, he had broken through into the lake. Later, they could fight it out on an almost equal basis.

The British, having seen the advantage of building ships inland, now proceeded to Isle aux Noix, way up on the Sorel River in Canada. There they began the construction of a frigate twice the size of the Yankee's *Saratoga*. An Indian agent brought word of this move to Macdonough and he called his ship builders together at Vergennes.

"Are we going to let them beat us to it?" he asked.

And the men shouted, "No! No! What do you want us to do?"

Macdonough spread before them a hastily sketched plan of a brig. "This is what I want—this ship—built, armed and ready to sail one month from today."

Cheering, the men rushed to the shops, forges and lumber sheds. Once again the forge and foundry belched smoke and flame as hammers clanged on white hot metal. Again showers of chips filled the air and once more the stillness was broken by the rasp and thud and clink of broad axe, adz and caulking iron.

The keel of the new brig was laid on July twenty-fifth and on the sixteenth of August Macdonough's miracle ship *Surprise* slid smoothly into the waters of Otter Creek. The Yankees had built, armed and launched a warship in less than three weeks!

* * * *

After Macdonough's brilliant exploit in bringing his new fleet down Otter Creek from Vergennes and out into the lake, and the quick building of the brig *Surprise*, the control of Champlain hung in the balance. Two fleets now sailed this narrow body of water; not until one or the other emerged victorious from battle would it be decided whether the British were to drive through to New York, or whether the Americans were to hold them at bay, confining them to their position in Canada.

The summer of 1814 passed with this issue hanging in the balance. The British were at the northern end of the lake, Macdonough at the southern, well knowing that the enemy must attack him or be stalemated. In September, word reached him that the British had set sail. He decided to await the attack in Plattsburg Bay, at anchor, with the head of his line of ships so near the shore that the enemy could not turn it; the other end of his line protected by shoals. With great foresight, Macdonough placed anchors and kedges so his vessels might be turned to face British fire from any angle.

With the *Saratoga*, the *Eagle*, the *Ticonderoga* and the *Preble* in a line backed up by his gun boats, he watched the British fleet stand bravely into the bay. Then, facing the battle that was to decide the fate of his country, Macdonough knelt on the deck with his officers, in a few moments of prayer. After that, quiet, as the men of the American fleet waited for the enemy's first fire.

The British opened first at extreme range, and all their shot fell short except one twelve pound ball which struck a hencoop aboard the *Saratoga*. From the shattered coop flapped a rooster, which perched on one of the American guns, spread his wings, arched his neck, and lustily crowed defiance. To the crews of the Yankee ships, this was a good omen, and they sent three roaring cheers echoing across the water.

Immediately the Americans opened with their first gun, a twenty-four pounder from the Saratoga, laid and sighted by Macdonough himself. The ball struck the British *Confiance* near the hawsehole and whistled down the deck, laying low several of the crew. All guns of both fleets now opened fire, commencing one of the most savage battles in naval history.

For hours the guns thundered and roared. Splinters flew, sails were ripped to shreds, yards and topmasts on both Yankee and British ships came crashing to the deck. Guns were dismounted, men fell. Aboard the *Saratoga* half the crew were casualties, but Macdonough fought on, directing the battle for the whole fleet; at the same time pointing and handling one of the long twenty-four pounders. A spar, smashed by British shot, fell on his head, knocking him out, but when he came to, he leaped to his feet and went on fighting. Shortly after, an enemy cannon ball clipped off the head of the captain of the next gun. The head flew through the air and caught Macdonough in the face, knocking him to the deck. Again he struggled to his feet, covered with gore, and went on with the fight, encouraging his men, directing them, observing the effects of the British fire, and still finding time to sight his favorite gun.

From this battle emerged two other names famous in our naval history. Aboard the *Ticonderoga*, young Hiram Paulding, age sixteen, captained one of the gun divisions. During the fight it was discovered that the slow matches for firing the guns were defective, seriously hampering the work of the broadside. This problem Paulding solved by ordering his men to fire pistols into the touch holes of the guns—and thus his battery stayed in the fight.

Lieutenant Cassin, the *Ticonderoga*'s captain, walked the taffrail while enemy shot whistled past him, encouraging his crew as they poured their fire at the steadily approaching British, who were planning to take his vessel by boarding. At last the enemy drew off, their attack broken, their boats full of wounded and dying men.

The thunderous battle roared on, and things were going badly, for the British fire had silenced every gun in the *Saratoga*'s starboard battery; twice, red-hot shot from the *Confiance* had set Macdonough's ship afire, and she was nearly a wreck. The *Eagle* was also in trouble, and all the Yankee gunboats had been driven off. Worse still, the British *Linnet* had got into position to rake the *Saratoga*, and her balls were tearing along the length of Macdonough's deck, doing terrific damage.

Now Macdonough's genius as a naval commander was more apparent than at any other time in the battle. The anchors and kedges he had carefully placed before the fight had been so located that now when his men rushed to the capstans and began walking them around to draw in the hawsers, the *Saratoga* slowly turned. Little by little she came about to face the British with her port broadside, undamaged and ready for action.

These new guns roared, the heavy shot ripped into the enemy. The *Confiance* began to settle; her guns were dismounted, her masts splintered, and she hauled down her flag. Immediately the men at the *Saratoga*'s capstans worked their ship to face the British *Linnet*, and pounded her into submission. The other enemy craft then either surrendered or limped away from the scene, leaking, their sails and rigging in tatters.

After two and a half hours of constant action, the battle was over. Macdonough was master of Lake Champlain. The British plan to split the United States by driving down the lake and down the Hudson River to New York City was knocked into a cocked hat. Had Thomas Macdonough and his men and his fleet failed on that September day in 1814, what would have followed? No one can say what the map of our country would look like today had the British prevailed.

Perhaps the folks we know as Vermont Yankees would be Canadian subjects, living under the Union Jack, and the children of the Green Mountain State would be learning to sing, "God Save the Queen." Hard to imagine? Sure, but it didn't happen, because Yankee Tom Macdonough built a fleet at Vergennes in forty days, got his vessels into Lake Champlain through the Dugway over night, and outsmarted and outfought the British at Plattsburg.

Molasses Disaster

ONE OF THE MOST unusual accidents ever to happen in New England was the molasses disaster in the North End of Boston in January 1919. Most folks call it the molasses *EXPLOSION*, but that is incorrect; the tank which held nearly three million gallons of molasses did not explode as many seem to think. It collapsed!

From the earliest days, molasses has been one of the most important commodities around the port of Boston. Billions of gallons have been shipped here from Cuba to be refined, but the crude molasses which arrived in January 1919 was not to be made into that savory stuff that is spread on bread for after-school sandwiches, nor was it for candy kisses. That molasses was to be distilled into alcohol by the Purity Distilling Company, an agency of the United States Alcohol Company, whose refining plant and storage tank were located at 529 Commercial Street in Boston's North End.

If you had been standing on historic Copp's Hill that January day, you could have looked right down on the scene of the disaster. Below was Commercial Street, a congested section of old wooden tenements and brick buildings bisected by the trestle of the Boston Elevated. On the harbor side of Commercial Street stood the warehouses of the Boston & Worcester and Eastern Massachusetts Street Railways, and the sheds of the Paving Division of the Public Works Department. Nearby stood the fire station and pier of "Engine 31," the fireboat, and anchored just off the Navy Yard was the training ship *Nantucket.*

Smack in the middle of this thickly congested area was the molasses tank, fifty feet tall, ninety feet across, and bulging with two million three hundred thousand gallons of crude molasses.

In contrast to the "below zero" weather of January 1917 and 1918, this week in mid-January 1919 was almost hot. Boston streets were dry and dusty, and on the Common a few spears of green grass could be seen. In the North End, kids played marbles and danced on the sidewalk to the tunes of a hurdy-gurdy. Two old-time residents of Commercial Street, Mrs. Clougherty and Mrs. O'Brien, leaned on the sills of their open windows to watch the hand-organ man and his monkey, and Mrs. Clougherty called to little Maria di Stassio to be careful as she crawled under some freight cars to gather firewood.

In the freight shed, the clerks were working in shirt sleeves, and bare-headed girls walked along the water front enjoying their lunch hour. The sailors who whistled at them carried their pea jackets on their arms and wished they were wearing whites, it was that springlike.

In the molasses refinery, Bill White shut off the pumps, washed up, and started up town to meet his wife for lunch. He bumped into Eric Blair, a driver for Wheeler's Express, and said, "Hiya Scotty! Thought you always et over in Charlestown."

"I do, Bill. In fact this is the first time in three years I've brought my lunch." And the Scotsman climbed onto the bulkhead and leaned back against the warm side of the molasses tank—for the first and last time.

In the Boston & Worcester freight terminal, foreman Percy Smerage was checking a pile of express bound for Worcester and Springfield: stack after stack of shoe boxes, bags of potatoes, bales of leather, barrels of beer, all kinds of stuff to be put into the freight car outside. Four of the freight cars were already loaded, the fifth was half empty, and as Smerage called to his assistant, a low, heavy rumble shook the neighborhood.

Then the noonday calm was shattered by an ear-splitting, snapping stacatto sound, like a thousand machine guns, followed by a booming roar as the great molasses tank split wide open at the base and a geyser of yellowish brown liquid shot sixty feet into the air, followed, as the crack in the tank widened, by a wave of molasses fifteen feet deep.

With a horrible, hissing, sucking sound, it splashed in a curving arc straight across Commercial Street, barely missing an elevated train, and crushing and engulfing everything and everybody in its path. The back-wash lifted the heavily loaded freight cars as if they were chips, and the half empty car was carried on the crest of the wave of molasses and sent crashing through the solid wall of the freight building. Instantly a seething sea of molasses burst into the terminal, tumbling the piles of stacked-up freight and trapping all the men working in the basement. Three of the clerks, in their checking booths, didn't have a chance because as the molasses rose to a depth of seven feet the floors collapsed, and everything fell into the cellar. In a matter of minutes, the basement and first floor were inundated to a depth of eleven feet, and in that swirling, sticky, sickish mess, men and horses died almost instantly.

When the tank burst apart, large sections were flung in all directions with such terrific force six of the steel supports of the elevated structure were sheered off, letting the overhead tracks drop into the street just a few seconds after a train had passed by.

The fronts of the Clougherty and O'Brien houses were sliced away as if by a sword, and two of the smaller dwellings were crushed like wads of waste paper. In the tangled wreckage of what had been her home, Mrs. Clougherty was found dead, and nearby in a deep pool of molasses was little Maria di Stassio.

On the ocean side of Commercial Street, the tidal wave of molasses struck the fire station, spinning it from its foundation and pushing it against some pilings where it leaned at a rakish angle. Three of the crew were killed outright: two firemen were blown through partitions, and engineer Lehay of "Fireboat 31" was crushed to death by a flying billiard table. The other firemen, under command of Captain Krake, worked heroically in spite of injuries to pull victims from under wagons, trucks, debris.

A cadet from the training ship *Nantucket* led a rescue squad to the third story gable of a house, which had been blown off and was floating on the lake of molasses. As they reached the gable, a little old lady leaned out her window and waved to them, apparently none the worse for her trip through the air.

I remember that day very well. I was at that time attached to the Office of Military Chief, 1st Naval Dist. Headquarters, in the Little Building. I had just emerged from a Tremont Street store with a brand new pair of shoes when Ladder 26 went by followed by other red wagons; I reported to my office and was immediately ordered to Commercial Street to make such photographs as might be valuable for the Navy files.

Never have I seen such a shambles, the whole area plastered with molasses. It slid from the rooftops, gurgled out of doors and windows, dripped from trees and overhead wires, and in the middle of Commercial Street, the molasses was five feet deep. As I started to go around this lake my foot slipped, and I went down with a splash, but I managed to hold my graflex high and a couple of firemen pulled me out. I saved the camera, but my uniform, overcoat and brand new shoes were ruined.

There was so much confusion that day, it's hard to remember all that happened. I do recall the Red Cross and Salvation Army workers wading up to their knees in that sticky stuff, and the silent forms dragged from under the top of the tank and from basements nearby. Fifteen bodies were located before dark, and six others later after the cellars were pumped out. Hundreds tackled the streets with brooms, shovels, squeegees, or behind high-pressure hose streams, and where the streams of salt water hit the molasses it turned into frothy, foaming suds and blew through the air like a cloud of soap bubbles.

I recall seeing Chief of Police Mike Crowley conferring with Medical Examiner McGrath, and State Chemist Walter Wedger searching through the ruins for signs of sabotage, but not a trace of dynamite or other explosive was ever found.

It was days before Commercial Street was opened to traffic, and weeks before the Boston hospitals got rid of the sticky stains which covered everything. Months afterward you could still see molasses footprints in downtown Boston, and the smell of that stuff lingered even longer.

Naturally there was a great controversy over the cause of the so-called "blast." Many claimed that the warm weather had caused the molasses to expand, but if that had been true, the tank would have burst at the top, not at the bottom. The alcohol company stoutly maintained that some "outside force" such as a bomb had done the damage, and they spent $50,000 in expert witness fees trying to prove this claim, but investigators found evidence of faulty construction, and finally it became known that the tank had been grossly overloaded.

The State Police reported, "At the time of the collapse, more than two million three hundred thousand gallons of molasses was in that tank, and with a weight of eleven pounds to the gallon, a pressure of over two tons per square foot was exerted on the sides and bottom of the container, and ultimately the weak spots let go."

As a result of this accident, one hundred twenty-five law suits were filed against the alcohol concern, and when the hearings opened in Suffolk County Court House, Boston, there wasn't room enough for the lawyers and witnesses. So by mutual agreement, the number of attorneys was reduced from one hundred thirty-five to two, and the witnesses were whittled down to a mere three thousand. There were one thousand five hundred eighty-four exhibits offered, and it took fifty thousand sheets of paper to record the typewritten testimony. Never in the history of New England had so many engineers, experts, metallurgists and men of science been called to the witness stand. One of them (an authority on "how much structural strain a steel tank can stand before breaking") testified all day every day for three weeks, and frequently court did not adjourn until ten o'clock at night.

The hearings on the molasses disaster began in 1919, and exactly six years to a day, in 1925, they came to a close. The United States Alcohol Company was held responsible, and had to pay over one million dollars in damages. It was brought out at the trial that plans for this giant tank were "railroaded" through the Building Department, and that actually no rigid inspection of the tank was ever made; it had been *ASSUMED* that it was of first class construction. But somewhere along the line, someone slipped. Careless workmen made a mistake which wasn't discovered, and so twenty-one were killed, dozens injured, and a property loss of one million dollars was the result of the great molasses disaster of January 15, 1919.

Runaway Pond

When the pioneers came into the valleys of Vermont from the neighboring state of New Hampshire, they built grist and saw mills on the brooks and rivers, using the water-power to grind their corn into meal and saw their logs into lumber.

David Blodgett built his mill on the Barton River, and over in Glover, Aaron Wilson put up two mills and a blacksmith shop on a branch of the same stream. As time passed, other small industries sprang up in the vicinity of Barton and Glover, most of them depending on streams which had their source in Mud Pond, up in the hills in a wild and thickly-forested region.

As far as water was concerned, it was feast or famine. In early spring the streams ran wild, often carrying out the dams; by midsummer there wasn't enough water to turn a wheel. The only dependable water-power time was between April Fool's Day and the Fourth of July, and the mill men broke their backs making the best of it.

In the spring of 1810 there was a prolonged and unseasonable drought. Logs and grain piled up, and farmers and millers began to get worried. Aaron Wilson, accompanied by his son and his hound dog, spent one long June day exploring the wild territory around Mud Pond, and made a startling discovery! The next day he summoned his customers to the mill store.

"Guess you know why we can't grind and saw. We hain't got no water," he said, then slyly added, "but I have got an idee and a keg of rum to back it up."

Instantly, his audience was all ears.

"Dunno whether you men realize it or not, but, on the fur side, less than forty rod from Mud Pond, what's dry as dust, is the northern end of Long Pond, what's full of water. And furthermore, Long Pond is nigh onto ninety feet higher than little Mud.

"I've ben thinking," he continued slowly, "if some of you fellers was willin' to help me dig a ditch between them ponds, the water'd run down hill pretty fast. Soon's Mud Pond is filled, we can start sawin' and grindin'."

As an afterthought Aaron added, "You'd have to bring your own tools, but I'll be glad to furnish the . . . refreshments!"

Above the murmur of excited approvals came the protesting voice of James Jenness of Sheffield. "If you know what's good for ye, Aaron Wilson, ye'll leave things the way the Lord made 'em. If He had wanted Long Pond to dreen off north into Memphremagog, instead of south into Champlain, He'd arranged it that way. I'm AGIN any monkeyin' with the face of nature!"

The majority, however, moved toward the door, shouting, "Bring on the rum, we'll dig the ditch!"

Aaron was not to be hurried. "Not today," he said. "We want to give everybody a chance to help. How about next Wednesday?"

Almost to a man they shouted, "Yea! June sixth!" And then they all laughed, for back in their native state of New Hampshire that would be Election Day, and they still liked to celebrate it.

"Then June six it is!" Grabbing a battered tin horn from a pile on the counter, Aaron waved it for silence. "Before we break up, I want a few of you fellers who know that country up there to take along these here horns. When you get through the woods on the day we're agoin' to do our diggin', blow hard so the others can find the way. It's mighty thick up in there."

Loring Frost, Silas Wheeler, Spencer Chamberlain and a few more, each picked up a tin horn and went out of the store, tooting, practicing for the day when they would blow them to guide the others through the wilderness. David Blodgett, owner of a saw mill, drew James Jenness aside and whispered, "I don't like the looks of this any more'n you do. How they going to stop all that water, once it starts arunnin' down hill?"

June 6, 1810, dawned fair and clear—a day never to be forgotten in that section of Vermont!

Before daylight, men and boys were hustling through their chores by lantern light in order to get an early start for the digging bee. Some had to tramp miles through underbrush and rocky ravines, a few rode as far as they could on horseback. Boys carried lunch boxes and light tools, men shouldered heavy crowbars, picks and shovels.

Loring Frost, Isaac Stokes and Aaron Wilson, Jr. were the first to arrive and they all but blew their lungs out on the old horns. By eight-thirty that morning, sixty-one men and boys had gathered at the northern end of Long Pond where the "committee" had decided to begin digging.

Now, Long Pond was one and a half miles in length and three-quarters of a mile wide, and except along the shore where it was shallow, it was from fifty to one hundred feet deep. It covered more than three hundred acres of land, and if the engineer who surveyed the scene afterward got his figures right, Long Pond contained, on the morning of June 6, 1810, not less than 1,000,988,000 gallons of water! And, mind you, it was fifteen hundred feet above sea level!

The natural outlet was at the southern end, where in the town of Greensboro the headwaters of the Lamoille River rise, to flow south through a fertile valley, eventually emptying into Lake Champlain. The only spot on the entire shore not composed of solid rock was at the northern end where the waters were confined by a bank of gravel which rose gently a few feet, then gradually sloped away for about five rods, descending rapidly thereafter from eighty to one hundred feet into the valley below. In the valley lay Mud Pond.

The sandy bank was covered with small birches and bushes easily pulled out by the roots. The only tree requiring the use of an axe was a lone cedar which stood a few feet away from a rotted stump; between the cedar and the stump was a slight depression. Here the "engineers" planned to break through. The surrounding soil was loose and sandy, only an occasional root had to be chopped, and by mid-morning the canal to Mud Pond was completed.

"It didn't take us long," a farmer explained, "digging down hill. I'd say she varied from two to four feet wide."

At quarter of eleven all hands climbed the slope, sweating and anxious to tap the pond and the rum barrel. The workers, in a holiday mood, watched expectantly while a handful of men removed the last barrier. Shovelsful of sand and gravel were dug out and tossed aside, widening and lengthening the channel. As the ditch was deepened, the diggers hit a hard-packed layer of "frozen" gravel; they broke through this crust to let the water flow into the ditch. But it didn't! It just seeped into the ground and disappeared, the way sea water will when kids on a beach try to make it flow through sand.

Then, suddenly, both sides of the narrow canal crumbled and caved in, pitching three men up to their armpits in quicksand. They were literally pulled out by the hair. As friends jokingly brushed them off and helped to empty their mud-clogged boots, a youngster screamed, "Look! Look out there at the whirlpool!"

Sure enough, a few yards off shore the calm blue surface of Long Pond was agitated by a patch of greenish-brown suds which bubbled and seethed as if from a subterranean eruption. Gaining momentum as it moved counter-clockwise, the whirlpool rapidly widened and sucked logs and floating leaves into its yawning vortex. A pair of loons rising suddenly to the surface were caught in the whirling current and drawn down out of sight.

To get a closer view of this phenomenon, about forty men ran along the shore and jumped onto a huge raft of logs, one end of which was moored among the cattails. They had barely reached it when a low rumble shook the shoreline, and, glancing back, the men saw the banking upon which they had been standing, split wide open. Leaving the raft and scrambling pell-mell over the quaking shore, they dashed for higher ground, reaching safety just in time. By now, the bottom of the ditch had dropped out of sight, and with an indescribable roar a billion gallons of water broke loose and swept down the mountainside.

The runaway pond followed its man-made canal; it surged into Mud Pond and filled it twenty-five feet above its normal level, and then the water went tumbling down, following the course of the little stream, cutting deep gorges in the sides of the hill, loosening boulders and uprooting trees.

At first the men were too stunned to realize that their homes and families were in the path of the roaring flood. Then several of the younger men started on the dead run to give warning to the settlements. Spencer Chamberlain, who knew that part of the country well, was able to beat the onrushing water because debris piled up in the gorges, forming dams which temporarily halted the flood—until it again broke loose with renewed fury !

When Chamberlain reached Aaron Wilson's grist mill,

he yelled, "Run for your lives! The pond's broke loose! Run to the hills!" And he raced on.

Hearing the warning, the miller grabbed a bag of grain in each hand and set out. Then he saw the towering wall of water, dropped the grain and hastily climbed to the top of a ledge. The roar of unleashed waters was louder than a thousand express trains, and was punctuated by ear-splitting cracks as trees a foot thick snapped off with reports like cannon fire. As the miller watched, the wave swept twenty feet over his mill buildings. For a split second he saw a terrified horse struggling amid the wreckage; then the great mass of tangled trees, branches, boulders and smashed buildings moved on, more slowly, down the valley.

Not a trace of that mill machinery was ever seen again, and down through the years searchers have hunted in vain for the great stone grinding wheels of the grist mill. Their final resting place is as much a mystery today as it was in June, 1810.

As the flood swept into Glover it reached a pine-clad plain where the soil was light and loamy. Trees were torn out and borne away on the crest of the flood, leaving a smooth, almost perfectly flat ledge, afterward used for regimental musters.

At three o'clock that afternoon, after tearing through Glover, the flood reached Barton, covering the main road to a depth of twelve feet. A man and woman there, racing for higher ground, suddenly remembered their baby, left behind in his cradle, and rescued him just as the water poured over the door sill.

David Blodgett, who had been "agin" the whole business, was plowing his pasture when he heard the ominous rumble, and, guessing what had happened, he ran to his mill, removed what he could and sought safety with his family. All his buildings were carried away, with his herd of cattle, his sheep, pigs and poultry.

Solomon Dorr also did a "Paul Revere," galloping down the road to give the alarm, fortifying himself with slugs of brandy along the way. His shouts gave the schoolmarm a chance to lead her pupils to a nearby hill where townsfolk had gathered, among them old Granny Gould who kept knitting away on a pair of mittens as if nothing were happening. But Grampa Gould fussed and fumed because he had just set three pans of milk on the kitchen table and didn't want to lose all that good rich cream. When the old couple returned to their home next day, they found a foot of mud over everything except the pans of milk—the kitchen table had floated up to the ceiling and down again, and nary a drop of the precious cream was lost.

Long Pond had broken loose at eleven o'clock in the forenoon, and seven hours later its crest reached Lake Memphremagog, which is twenty-five miles away and north of the present site of Newport, Vermont. The average height of the water along its route was over six feet, but in some places, where debris piled up in gorges and ravines, the high-water mark was seventy feet!

All through the valley tens of thousands of fish were left flopping in the sun. In Coventry Falls, five tons of trout, salmon, suckers and eels were picked up, and bushels of bass and sunfish were salvaged from the muddy ooze.

In Glover village today, if you look at the underpinning of the Universalist church, you will see parts of a boulder eighteen feet long and seven wide and thought to weigh nearly one hundred tons, which was pushed more than a mile, landing finally near the center of the village. Stone masons split it up with wedges so it could be used as foundation for the church and several other buildings.

After the excitement died down, David Blodgett brought suit against those who were responsible for letting out the water from Long Pond; the case remained on the docket for two years but never came to trial.

It was naturally supposed for some years that the valley was entirely ruined for farming. In many places the land was covered with gravel and in others was buried under a layer of soft mud upon which neither man nor beast could stand. But this dried out, and a farmer who purchased one hundred acres of "waste land" for $1.00 an acre within three years had a crop of herdsgrass six feet tall. Then it was discovered this was some of the most fertile land in all Vermont!

Public sentiment changes with the passage of time, and on June 6, 1910, when the town of Glover, Vermont, commemorated the 100th anniversary of "Runaway Pond," the pioneers who plundered the pond were hailed as heroes. As a fine granite marker on the site of Long Pond was unveiled, the orator of the day exclaimed, "Unwittingly, those early citizens remedied a dangerous situation with comparatively little damage and no loss of life. Had Long Pond remained until now and had broken through its banks in modern times, the damage would have run into millions and the Lord only knows how many thousand might have been killed."

And so ends the story of men who were pioneers in "monkeying with the face of nature."

Presque Isle Lynching

In the days when Aroostook County, Maine, was truly a howling wilderness, winter came early and stayed late. There was always snow for sleighing at Thanksgiving, much more snow by Christmas, and the long, rugged months of January, February and March were marked by below zero temperatures, blizzard after blizzard, and the wildest of winter weather.

Not until the first warm showers of April melted the deep snow did the roads become bare in spots and covered with slush the rest of the way. For weeks the going was so bad that farmers' wagons labored in mud at times up to their hubs; and the crusted snow lay deep in the fields and the forest.

Such were conditions in Aroostook County in late April, 1873, when a no-good character named James Cullen broke into Dave Dudley's store at Ball's Mills (now Mapleton) and helped himself to some canned goods and a plug of chewing tobacco. Big, clumsy and red headed, Cullen was well known in the logging camps along the Border and across the line in Canada. Summer and fall he worked for the potato growers; winter and spring found him in the woods, his mighty arms wielding his woodsman's axe with the strength of ten men. His stolid, stupid face was framed with a mass of flaming red whiskers and he was famous for having the biggest pair of feet in those parts.

Between Mapleton and Presque Isle, a man named John Swanbeck lived alone in a log cabin. Most of the time he hunted and fished, but during the winter months he earned a few dollars by cutting and shaving shingles in his cabin which stood in a clearing at the edge of Chapman's Woods. Ever since 1873, this place has been called the "Bloody Half Acre."

On the afternoon of April twenty-ninth, Swanbeck had finished his work and was tying his shingles into bundles when he saw a big man, lurching toward the cabin on snowshoes. From the way he swaggered, and from his red beard and hair, he instantly recognized Cullen. Cullen came straight toward the cabin, kicked off his snowshoes and entered without knocking.

"What's the hurry, Jim?" Swanbeck asked. "You look like the Devil was after you."

"He is—that devil of a deputy sheriff Granville Hayden. And he's got some other men with him. Says I swiped some canned stuff from Dudley's store, when all I took was a plug of terbaccy." He stacked his snowshoes behind the wood box, sat down and rubbed his swollen right ankle.

"I'd been across the Border long ago if I hadn't hurt my foot. Aches like hell and I'm plumb tuckered out."

Swanbeck's woodsman's instinct to shelter and help any man in trouble came to the fore, and he hastened to say, "That's too bad. Why don't you bunk here for the night, then you can be over the Line by early tomorrow?" (It was a common practice to let petty thieves and criminals get out of the country into Canada, thus saving the State of Maine the expense of court procedure.)

While John Swanbeck fried some potatoes and made a pot of tea, Cullen sat by the window watching the road and rubbing his ankle. Outside, the low-hanging clouds hung heavy with a promise of additional snow.

After a meager meal, the two men sat and smoked, then Cullen dragged a mattress toward the fire and was soon snoring lustily. Swanbeck lay in his bunk, for a while wondering if he had done right in harboring this thief; then he dropped off to sleep. When morning came, it was snowing lightly so Swanbeck let Cullen sleep while he built up the fire, mixed batter for flapjacks and put on the coffee pot. Finally they ate, mostly in silence; then Swanbeck straddled his wooden "horse" and began shaving shingles while Cullen sat by the fire. He made no move to be on his way, and sympathetic Swanbeck did not urge him.

It was late afternoon when Swanbeck knocked off work, picked up a pail and went to the well for water. The snow had stopped, the sun had come out, and a warm spring glow filled the clearing. From far off came the sound of voices, and then, moving among the slender birches in the distance, Swanbeck saw three men, each carrying a rifle.

One was Sheriff Granville Hayden, who hollered, "You got plenty of snow in here for this late in the season, John!" And as he came forward and extended his hand, he said cautiously, "And a good thing for us; we followed Cullen's tracks all the way in. If he's in the cabin, I have a warrant to take him back." Swanbeck nodded and lowered his pail into the well. The other two men, Bill Hubbard from Castle Hill and Minot Bird from Presque Isle, watched Hayden as he strode toward the log cabin.

No one will ever know what passed between the sheriff and the man he was after, but it is to be assumed that Cullen admitted his petty theft and agreed to go back to town and face the charges, for both men were smiling when the others went in to get warm and to rest.

The sheriff, his boots drying in front of the fire, said, "John, I'm going to ask a favor, not so much for me as for the others. Both Bill, here, and young Bird, aren't used to tramping in the snow, and they're mighty tired, and my prisoner seems to have a badly sprained ankle. If you could put us up for the night, we could all rest and make a fresh start in the morning."

"Why, sure," Swanbeck said, "sure thing. But you'll have to eat flapjacks and salt pork, 'cause that's all I got."

Being fagged out, they turned in early. Cullen curled up in his corner, while the others good-naturedly pitched pennies to see who would occupy the single bunk. Bird and Swanbeck won the toss, so Hayden and Bill Hubbard pulled some blankets in front of the fire and slept on the floor.

Four of the five men were soon snoring lustily; only James Cullen was wide awake, planning his next move. Although he had confessed to his crime and agreed to go back with the sheriff, he had no such thought in his mind right now. Somehow, he must get rid of his captors and escape across the Border. The simplest thing would have been to get up and walk out while the others were fast asleep. With good luck he could have been in Canada in a few hours. Instead, Cullen waited till he could hear all four men snoring, then he arose, crossed to the fire, and kicked at the logs. None of the men awoke, so he tossed on a log. That didn't awake them either; this was the time to strike—and fast! Grabbing Swanbeck's double-edged axe, Cullen crossed to where Sheriff Hayden and Hubbard lay, and with two mighty blows he crushed their skulls. Then he limped toward the bed to kill Swanbeck and Bird.

Swanbeck had awakened at the sound of the blows; in the semi-darkness, he saw Cullen move toward him, and instantly he reached for a door beside his bunk and snatched it open just as the weapon swung at him. The axe went crashing through the door and stuck there. Swanbeck scrambled out of his bunk, clawing around for the sheriff's rifle, but Cullen found it first. Covering both Swanbeck and Bird, he said, "If you want to live, pile some shingles on that fire, and drag in some brush."

Then Cullen stepped back and hauled first one, then the other, of the lifeless forms of the men he had murdered, into the open fireplace.

"Come on!" he ordered. "This has got to be a hot fire."

With the crazy man threatening to shoot at any moment, Swanbeck and Bird pulled off spruce limbs and piled great armfuls on top of the corpses. In no time, the spruce boughs sizzled and sang, and the shingles snapped and cracked. A sudden puff of smoke and flame filled the room and poured outside where it rose in a tall column into the crisp morning air, to be edged with gold by the rising sun.

Swanbeck heard Cullen cough, and, seeing him wipe his reddened eyes, he whispered to Bird. "Let's run for it before he can see to shoot!" And off they dashed in their stocking feet over the crusted snow. At last Cullen saw them and fired three shots. He missed, and the two men plunged on through the snow. Once on the main road (between Mapleton and Presque Isle) they ran as fast as they could, stumbling over the frozen ruts until at last they turned in at the Garland farm.

The Garlands were sitting down to breakfast when they heard Swanbeck yell, "Help! Get your guns and get back to my place! Jim Cullen's gone crazy! He's killed Sheriff Hayden and Bill Hubbard, and he'll kill us if he can!"

There were no telephones then, and traveling on the backwoods roads was slow, but inside of two hours, Garland and his farmhands had rounded up two dozen men, and with Minot Bird leading the way, they struck through the woods till they came to Cullen's bloody footprints in the snow. Then they saw where he had put on his snow shoes and headed for his own home on Haystack Mountain.

News of the double murder spread rapidly and by midafternoon an angry crowd of Aroostook citizens, led by Collamore Griffin, reached the story-and-a-half house where Cullen lived. They quickly surrounded it, each man with a club or gun; and they vowed to each other that Cullen would pay for his crimes in short order. At the first command to "come out!" Mrs. Cullen, a wild, unkempt looking woman, stuck her frowsled head from an upstairs window and hollered back.

"What do you want? James? Why he hain't been here for three days. Went to Canada, lookin' for work."

But just then, one of the boys came running from the back of the house to tell the leader of the posse, "There's bloody footprints out back . . . . by the cellar door!"

While the men kept their guns leveled at the house, other boys were sent to the barn to fetch armfuls of hay, which they piled around the doors, front and back, and into the bulkhead leading to the cellar. Kindling wood and sticks from the woodpile were tossed on top, and then Collamore motioned for all to stop and be silent.

Cupping his hands to his mouth, he shouted, "You better come out, Cullen, we know you are in there! Come out with your hands over your head."

He waited, but the only response was the whining voice from the upstairs window as Cullen's wife yelled, "I tell you, there's no one here but me. Jim went away three days ago."

Somehow this statement carried little or no conviction, and one of the men, at a nod from Collamore, rolled some hay and birch bark into a torch, lighted it with a match and marched toward the hay-filled bulkhead.

"This is your last chance, Cullen," Collamore shouted, "Come out or be roasted alive!" And the man moved forward with the blazing torch. As he bent over to set the hay ablaze, the door flew open and Cullen, haggard, wild-eyed, frightened, came out with his hands over his scraggly head. A score of guns aimed at his heart.

"Stop!" he yelled. "Don't shoot! All I did was take a few cans of beans."

"You killed Sheriff Hayden and Hubbard," someone snapped.

To this, Cullen growled, "I didn't either. That was Swanbeck's idea." But before he could say more, he was grabbed, tied up, hustled into a wagon, and with five men practically on top of him, the murderer was driven to Mapleton, where already an excited crowd had gathered.

There being no jail, Cullen was taken to the very store he had robbed, and in the rear of the building where bags of grain were kept, he was tied and chained to an upright post, his captors sitting in a circle, armed and ready to pounce if he made the slightest move.

When the constable arrived to question Cullen, he readily admitted the killings, and snarled with bravado, "And I would have killed the others if I had the chance."

Deputies were soon dispatched to search the smouldering ruins of Swanbeck's cabin, and late that night they returned with what evidence they could find: the blood-stained, double-edged woodsman's axe, the sheriff's badge, and a salt box filled with charred bones.

A farmer, staring at the gruesome display said sadly, "So that's all that's left of Sheriff Hayden."

Cullen grinned sarcastically and cackled, "He looks nice, don't he?"

No one replied, but many a man, with smouldering anger, remembering the brutal slaying of the Hontvet women on lonely Smutty Nose Island a few months before, vowed that James Cullen was not to be treated as gently as Louis Wagner had been. The party broke into small groups, and with knowing gestures and sly winks they whispered and nodded, and finally drifted out of the store. Only a deputy sheriff and three other men remained to guard Cullen, chained to his stanchion.

All that afternoon men and boys could be seen riding "up hill and down dale" to hold brief whispered conversations with grim-faced farmers who had known Sheriff Hayden and liked him. Many a farmer's wife was surprised to hear her husband say, "I'd like supper early tonight; got to go to a special meetin'." The sun went down and it got cold. Long shadows filled the valley, lights came on in the houses along the country roads, and lanterns flashed from the wagons and saddles of two hundred men.

About an hour after dark, Cullen, tied hand and foot, was taken from Dudley's store and lifted into a wagon. Guarded by Constable B. J. Hughes and six deputies, he started his journey to the jail in Presque Isle.

But he was less than a mile out of Mapleton when the wagon was halted by a group of men with handkerchiefs over their faces. While these unknown men formed a circle around the constable's wagon, five others jumped from their horses, grabbed Cullen and pulled him to the ground. The circle around them parted to let them pass, and they moved into the woods without a word.

Coming to a grove of maple trees, they halted and quickly tossed around Cullen's neck one end of a stout rope with a slip noose. Before he had time to protest, the rope was drawn tight, and the murderer was dangling from a limb of the maple tree. Only a dozen actually had hold of that rope, but years afterward, whenever the story of this crime was told, many a respectable man "let on" that either he—or his dad or his aging grandfather—had had a hand in the execution.

After a quarter of an hour had passed, Dr. Parker, who had ridden over in the wagon with Cullen, was asked to step forward to see if he was dead. The good country physician felt of Cullen's lifeless wrist and said quietly, "He must be dead, but let's leave him hang a mite longer to be sure."

Just before sunrise Cullen's corpse was cut down, put in a hastily made wooden box and carted to Presque Isle, where on the south side of State Street it was placed on display in Fred Barker's general store. All business was suspended, with many of the stores in town closing so that clerks could go have a look at the man who had killed the sheriff. A constant line of curious people, both young and old, filed past the window by day and by night, then went to get something to eat, and came back to stand in line and have another look. Whole families, it is said, drove into Presque Isle from outlying towns, some coming across the border from Canadian communities where the scoundrel Cullen was known as a bad character and Sheriff Hayden as a man of honor.

It was agreed by a committee in charge that Cullen should be buried in an unmarked grave, and after much wrangling as to which spot should be thus defiled, somebody suggested the center of the town dump. There, with only a few to witness, the box bearing Cullen's remains was carried at night. A deep hole was dug, and the body dumped among the rocks, dirt, tin cans and garbage.

Many a man in that section of Maine, world famous for its potatoes, claimed he knew the exact spot where murderer Cullen was buried in secret, but when we tried to locate it a few years ago, we found that it had been leveled over to make a runway. You see, James Cullen's bones—what's left of them—are now part of the Presque Isle airport.

Justice Herbert T. Powers of the Maine Superior Court, knew a lot about this case and helped me get the facts. When a young lawyer, Judge Powers attended a lecture on phrenology by "Professor" Luther Bateman, who hinted it was Cullen's skull he used in his demonstrations.

And somewhere up in Aroostook, there's another gruesome relic of the Cullen-Hayden-Hubbard tragedy: a short length of rope with a few red whiskers still sticking to the noose near the hangman's knot.

Well, that's the story of Maine's lynching, and the only one I ever heard of in New England.

Ruth Blay

ALMOST EVERY New England community has had at least one unforgettable event, a fire, flood, shipwreck or murder, which people have remembered and talked about for years. On the other hand, some startling incidents, like the grave robberies in Essex, Massachusetts, and the Ruth Blay case in Portsmouth, New Hampshire, which greatly shocked the populace at the time, have been practically forgotten.

I first heard of the Ruth Blay case years ago; I looked it up in the Boston Public Library, and checked with what accounts I could find, but because I didn't have enough facts to fill a broadcast, I laid my notes away. Then I received a note from Charles N. Dennett, Jr. of South Hampton, New Hampshire, saying he had been collecting information and documents on this sensational case, and if I cared to call, he would let me go through them.

So I dropped in on Charles Dennett, and got quite a surprise. He was not middle-aged as I had assumed, but a clean-cut young man of seventeen, just out of highschool and very much interested in local history. He lived with his parents in a fine, one-hundred-year-old farm house almost opposite the old homestead from which Ruth Blay was dragged off to jail charged with the murder of her only child.

In 1768, when this scandal shook the countryside, Ruth Blay, a local school teacher, was boarding with the Clough family in South Hampton. She was in her early twenties; a tall, quiet young lady from a fine family of nearby farming folks.

In June of that year one of the farm hands on the Clough place stumbled upon the body of a dead child wrapped in a blue quilt, and in a small hamlet like South Hampton such a gruesome discovery was almost catastrophic.

At that time New Hampshire was a Royal Province governed by John Wentworth, nephew of the first Royal Governor Benning Wentworth. All laws were of course English laws, and the penalty for concealing the birth, or death, of an illegitimate child was DEATH! The king's officers were relentless in their investigations, and suspicion soon fell on the shoulders of Ruth Blay. After considerable questioning the young school teacher tearfully but without shame admitted the baby was hers, but she stoutly denied having caused its death. Broken hearted and alone with her grief, she had hidden the dead infant in Mr. Clough's barn until such time as she could give it proper burial.

Miss Blay was placed under arrest, and taken by Sheriff

Packer to the Portsmouth jail to await the findings of a coroner's jury.

Among the papers which Mr. Dennett showed us was an original summons served on the persons of Isaiah Bartlett, Abish Cooper, William Rowell and Jeremy Webster, all friends and neighbors of the Clough family, to present themselves at the inquest to give "such evidence as you may know regarding an action between our Sovereign Lord and King and Ruth Blay." Actually these good folks of South Hampton knew nothing of the circumstances except that the body of a child in a blue quilt had been found in the Clough's barn, but that was enough. When the hastily convened inquest adjourned, its verdict shocked the countryside.

"The Jury finds," said the coroner, "that the dead child belonged to Ruth Blay and that it met its death by violence."

Poor Ruth stoutly denied the charge and insisted over and over that her baby was still-born. Nevertheless Sheriff Packer marched Ruth back to her dreary cell in the Portsmouth jail to await trial in September. A few of Ruth's intimate friends got together and sent a petition to Governor Wentworth, but as the weeks went by with no word from His Excellency, Ruth gave up all hope of clemency.

When such a thing happens today—and it has happened more than once—the accused is given every chance to prove her innocence, and if the accused cannot afford an attorney, the best legal talent is furnished by the state, but in those tyrannical times, no such legal aid, or help of any kind, was forthcoming for Ruth Blay. Instead, the government lined up the most able legal lights of the Province, and Wiseman Claggett, the King's Attorney, was put in charge of the prosecution. Educated in England and trained in the courts of London where such cases for the Crown gave ample opportunity for elocution, Wiseman Claggett made a profound impression on the jurors.

Tall, robust and attired in full regalia, the King's Attorney was an imposing figure. He knew all the tricks. He flattered the jury, used highfaultin' phrases, raised his bushy brows and curled his thin lips in scorn as he pictured Ruth Blay, "the blackest kind of criminal," a heartless mother who had murdered her own child. Most of the townspeople didn't like all this bluster and table-thumping, but as all the evidence, circumstantial though it was, was against the unfortunate school teacher, the jury had to bring in a verdict of GUILTY!

It doesn't take much imagination to picture that crowded courtroom as Ruth Blay was ordered to stand and receive sentence; the white-faced clerk, turning to Sheriff Packer, intoned: "We command you, therefore; that on Thursday the 24th day of November between the hours of twelve o'clock noon and two of the clock of the same day you carry the said Ruth Blay from a jail in Portsmouth where she is now in your custody to the place of execution and cause her the said Ruth Blay to then and there be hanged by her neck till her body be dead."

Only a few stifled sobs broke the breathless stillness of the courtroom as the clerk continued: "Hereof fail not. And for your sodoing this shall be your sufficient warrant. When you have executed this writ make proper return thereof with your doings thereon unto the clerk's office of an Superior Court of Judicate. By Order of the Court George Third King in the 8th year of our Reign Sept. 3rd. A. Dominee 1768."

Now I have known quite a number of sheriffs in my day, and without exception they have been jovial kind-hearted County officials always ready to give the under dog a break. But Sheriff Thomas Packer wasn't cut from that kind of comforting cloth. Besides being wealthy and pompous he was selfish and cold blooded. He strutted around Portsmouth enjoying the importance that had fallen on him as Lord High Executioner, and he warned all who talked about a reprieve. "It will do no good whatsoever to seek a pardon for this hard-hearted criminal, this murderer of her own child. His Excellency may postpone for a few days or even weeks, but mark me, Ruth Blay will hang, never fear."

Governor Wentworth did postpone the execution from November twenty-fourth to December thirtieth, and hope ran high among Ruth's friends, who kept sending petitions to the executive mansion. But as the day of the execution drew near and the country roads were filled with whole families who came from miles away to witness the hanging, Ruth Blay lost all hope.

The loyal friends who visited Ruth in jail tried to comfort her by saying, "Governor Wentworth has a kind heart. He'll grant a reprieve, wait and see."

And he did, on the very morning the execution was to take place.

I have often wondered how many of the summer tourists

driving back and forth between New Castle, Rye Beach and Portsmouth realize they are passing the place where almost two hundred years ago a gallows stood on a ridge of land in the South Parish pasture. It looks right down on the road to Little Harbor, and later became known as the Auburn Street cemetery. When I visited there, the Superintendent of the cemetery showed me where more than one thousand men, women and children—if you can imagine such a thing—gathered on that bright December day in 1768 for the purpose of watching an innocent young woman pay with her life for a crime which the Crown said she had wilfully committed.

All of the accounts that we have been able to uncover say it was a clear, crisp winter morning, with very little snow, when Ruth Blay was assisted from her cell in the Portsmouth jail and placed in a horse-drawn cart to be driven to the shore pasture where a multitude had gathered around the gallows.

At Ruth's request, she was allowed to put on, for the solemn occasion, a new and very lovely silk dress. "Much better and more expensive," the papers said, "than most brides of that day could afford." But this was of little comfort to the grief-stricken and terrified young school teacher who could not know as she rode along like Joan of Arc, that at that very moment John Wentworth was affixing his name to a reprieve to be delivered by messenger. So Ruth Blay wept and wailed, "so loud and heart-rending," said one old lady, "everyone heard her and prayed."

As I said, whole families drove in from remote points with lunch baskets and babes in arms. Farmers left their fields and woodchopping; shops were closed and ships idle. Children too young to know what it was all about scampered with barking dogs among the snow-sprinkled trees or played hide-and-go-seek among the stacks of piled up grain, while their elders waited with fast beating hearts for the sight they did not really want to see yet dared not miss, scheduled for high noon or soon thereafter.

As the cart reached the foot of the hill and started up, a deep-throated murmur rose from the crowd, then instant silence, broken by the shouts of some young men high in the trees a short distance away. They had caught a brief glimpse of a hatless rider dashing down the frosty Pike, and intuition told them the urgency of his mission. "The reprieve!" they shouted, but the creak of cart wheels, barking dogs, and the sudden raucous voice of Sheriff Packer drowned out the glad tidings.

The sheriff pushed his bulk through the crowd and said testily, "Make way for the law! Let's get this over with. Make way there . . ."

One man tapped the sheriff on the shoulder to remind him it was only a "bit past ten o'clock," but the impatient official only glared and snarled, "It'll be way past my dinner time when I get home, and I'm accustomed to having my meals on time."

Then he turned to the driver. "Fetch that cart up under the rope, and be quick about it!"

The messenger bringing the precious paper bearing the signature of Governor John Wentworth, which would spare the life of Ruth Blay, was now only a short distance away, and realizing the time of the execution had been officially set, as everyone knew, between the "hour of twelve noon and two o'clock of the same day" he had plenty of time, so he slowed down, and besides, there was such a crowd he had to find a place to tether his horse, and fairly fight his way up the slope.

On the crest of the hill, Sheriff Packer had already waved the crowd into silence, and as every eye followed his every move, he strode to the cart, jerked Ruth Blay to her feet, flung the noose over her bare head and bluntly commanded, "Ruth Blay, before you go to your doom, look ye for the last time upon the sea and the land which encompasses it." And he said some other things which have been lost to posterity, and when he had finished his harangue, he gave the rope a final hitch and nodded to the driver to pull away the cart.

Cries of horror suddenly arose from the crowd. "Hold, Sheriff! Hold! 'Taint time yet. Wait! Wait!" and at that moment the messenger was manfully pushing his way through a seething mass of hysterical humanity, never realizing what was about to happen just a few hundred feet above him.

They were still shouting, "HOLD! WAIT!" when he broke through and ran toward the gallows, but Sheriff Packer wouldn't wait.

"Drive on!" he bellowed. "Get that cart going. I'm in a hurry!"

The horses started, stumbled, the cart wheels creaked and the rope tightened, and the messenger, hardly able to comprehend what he was seeing, shouted, "Stop! Stop! I bring the governor's pardon . . ." but unfortunately for Ruth

Blay, his voice was drowned in the general uproar, and by the time he reached the gallows, it was too late.

Old time accounts say that crowd became a howling mob, shrieking for vengeance. They tore the gallows apart, and lugged the lumber to the front of the sheriff's house, where it was piled and burned. They tramped down the nearby grain, stoned the sheriff's windows and spattered his big white residence with mud and snowballs, and as darkness came on the angry citizens shouted, "Lynch the Tory! String him up as he did Ruth Blay."

But the only figure to swing, from an improvised gallows in the street of Portsmouth that night, was a straw-filled dummy, an effigy of Sheriff Packer on which a placard was pinned bearing these words:

"Am I to lose my dinner?
This woman for to hang?
Come draw away the cart, boys
And don't stop to say Amen."

Ruth Blay was the last woman to be hanged for crime in New Hampshire, and the first to be buried in the huge Auburn Street Cemetery, at the foot of the hill on which she died.

The Legend of Micah Rood

MANY YEARS AGO, in what is now the town of Franklin, Connecticut, there lived a mean, lazy and inhospitable hermit named Micah Rood. He was a tall, thin, wiry man, with permanent stubble of beard and small, black, beady eyes which narrowed into mere slits whenever he chanced to see something he wanted. Micah dressed shabbily, and the small log shack he lived in was poorly furnished. The living room had only a table, two chairs, the broken-down stove he cooked on and an apology for a bed.

In one corner, there was a large sea chest where, presumably, Micah kept his valuables. The one window, which looked out onto the garden, lacked several panes of glass, and in winter was stuffed with rags to keep out the driving snow and sleet.

Attached to the shack was a small shed which in turn led

to the pig pen. This log shack stood on a side hill, just in front of a stand of thick woods, and was within the boundaries of what became the Ayer farm, which, incidentally, was for many years the oldest piece of New England real estate to be owned and occupied by one family.

The one beautiful thing Micah did possess was an apple tree. In the spring time, it was a mass of fragrant, snow-white blossoms, and in the fall its gnarled branches bent to the ground with ripe fruit—not the big, red, juicy apples we have today, for those were unknown in the old days—most apple trees then (and this was in the days before Johnny Appleseed) bore very poor fruit, just little, hard, sour nubbins. But Micah's apples were bigger and better than the average, and as has happened from time immemorial, small boys frequently climbed the stone wall to fill their pockets when the hermit wasn't looking. Sometimes, mean old Micah, wrapped in a dingy sheet, made the youngsters' blood run cold as he moaned and whined from the shadows of the slanting tombstones of the graveyard nearby.

One year Samuel Picket filled his pockets, and after pressing the apples on his mother for a prized apple pie, he placed the hardest and greenest apple in an upstairs bureau drawer, along with a last year's robin's nest and some striped stones, found in the brook, which he used for curing warts. He hoped the apple would become eatable, but instead of ripening, it just shriveled, into a hard, woody lump, its outer skin much wrinkled. The lad didn't know it, but strange forces were at work, to make that old, dried apple, the clue to a heinous crime!

Twice each year, once in the spring and again before winter set in, Micah Rood had a visitor named Old Solomon, a peddler, a bent and benign character who walked cross country with a bag on his back filled with knickknacks, toys and tinware. He was a kind of philosophical "furriner" and his wrinkled and pathetic old face wreathed in smiles whenever anyone had a kind word for him.

Solomon the peddler was passionately fond of flowers, especially the first blossoms of spring, and when he arrived at Micah's place around the first of each May, he would revel in the yellow cowslip he saw in the meadow brooks, and the delicate blooms of the shad bush, and if Micah Rood's apple tree happened to be in full bloom, he'd ease the heavy pack from his lop-sided shoulder, slump onto the bench by the door and feast his travel-weary eyes on the mass of snow white blossoms, which stood out sharply against the bare, brown earth and bright blue sky.

After a drink from the rusty tin dipper, Solomon would fill his pipe and stroll out to stand under that apple tree, listening enraptured to the buzz of the bees, and he would smile like a child when a chance breeze wafted a shower of white petals around him.

"Dey are beaUtiful! BeaUtiful!" he would say, softly, and later, when the setting sun bathed the tree with a pink glow, Solomon would sit spellbound, drinking in the beauty and perfume.

Now the miser bought very little from Old Solomon—occasionally a paper of pins or a packet of snuff, and once in a great while a tin dish or two; but he did permit the pack-peddler to stay over night. The miser's frugal fare was quite enough for Solomon, and over a period of years the two strange characters became almost friends.

One spring the peddler arrived earlier than was his custom, and as he toiled up the path, Micah, watching from his rocking chair by the window, noted that Old Solomon had aged. He was thinner and haggard, and as he sat down and removed his heavy pack, Micah saw the old man's hands shake, and in the peddler's eyes, there was the unmistakable look of . . . . TERROR.

As usual, the miser whined about his hard luck, the unseasonable weather, and the barrenness of his rocky pasture, but Solomon, with bowed head, gave thanks for his blessings: the friendship of good Mr. Rood, and the fact that just the night before, he had been spared from a brutal beating by a band of roustabouts in a wayside tavern.

Curious, Micah Rood asked leading questions, and when the peddler produced a small bag, held around his neck by a stout cord, and patted it fondly, the hermit's eyes narrowed, and his claw-like hands clinched, so eager was he to find out what was in the little bag.

By dint of hard work, shrewd bargains and weary miles of travel on foot, Solomon had amassed what was for those times a good-sized fortune—not in gold, which makes men greedy, nor in silver, which is heavy to carry, but in diamonds—and in that little pouch he had some of the largest and most sparkling gems Micah Rood had ever seen.

Usually, Micah didn't light a candle for his evening meal; they were too costly to come by. But this night, he produced a stump of wax set into a bottle, and lighted it, and as he went to bolt the door and draw the curtain, he noted that outside it had begun to snow. By the time the two men had finished their supper, the wind had risen, it was snowing faster, and darkness had already engulfed the lonely log shack.

Again, Micah cursed the late spring snow storm, but Old Solomon shook his shaggy head and smiled. " 'Twill be good for the garden. 'Poor man's manure' we call it in the old country," and as he unfastened his coat before retiring, he removed the bag of diamonds to put them under his pillow.

Controlling his voice as best he could, the miser said, "Let's look at what you have in that pouch again, Solomon. I like to see fancy things. Sort of cheers me up."

The peddler hesitated, looking around the dingy room. "Your door . . . is it locked securely?" And he turned so his shadow from the sputtering candle would cover the table. Then with fingers that trembled he unfastened the cord, and from the well-worn pouch he poured out a handful of gleaming stones. In the light of the candle, they glowed and sparkled with their own flash and fire.

Micah Rood sucked in his breath, and thought greedily, "If I had those, I'd never have to work again—no more ploughing and planting, no more feeding pigs. I could live in ease and comfort." His deep-lined face was hard and cunning while the peddler's wore a soft and kindly expression.

As Solomon scooped up the diamonds and dropped them into the pouch, he whispered confidentially, "Last night, at the Blue Anchor Tavern, I almost lost them, and my life too." He jumped as an outside door banged.

" 'Tis but the wind," said Micah, "go on, tell me what happened."

"I vas sleeping in the shed at the tavern, and something vaked me. I felt hands trying to get at my pouch, but I screamed and the teefs ran away in the dark." He swallowed hard, and the same look of terror which Micah had noted before, came into his eyes. "I am scared, friend Rood, for I tink those ruffians have followed me."

He looked around again, shaking with fright. "Dey would not stop to kill an old man to get these." And he held the pouch tight against his bosom. "But," he said, taking a long deep breath, " 'Twill do them no good, for on them I have put the curse, the curse I learned in the old country."

Micah wasn't listening; he was gazing into the dark recesses of his shack, and everywhere he looked, he saw diamonds, and dollars, and thought of a selfish life of ease and luxury. Outside the wind moaned louder, the wind whipped the trees and wet snow slashed against the few remaining panes of glass.

Finally, he blew out the candle and both men stretched out in the darkness.

Solomon was soon snoring, but Micah couldn't get the diamonds out of his mind. He knew the peddler would be up and on his way, as he always was, long before daybreak. So, he stayed awake, listening to the gnawing of the rats in his shed, and then to the satisfying sound of dripping water as the snow turned to rain. Micah was glad, for snow holds footprints which rain washes away, and footprints can be dangerous sometimes.

* * * *

The next morning, all the snow had gone except one small patch around Micah's apple tree, and that patch was stained with blood—the blood of the old peddler. Nearby was his pack with its toys and tinware scattered in the melting slush. The rain had washed away all the footprints—except those of the terrified lad who, hastening to do his early morning chores, had stumbled on Solomon's body, face down under the apple tree.

Naturally, he ran to the nearest house, which was Micah's, and, rousing the miser, he told of his gruesome find. Micah was quite upset (as he had a right to be!) but when questioned by the county officers, Micah could offer no solution to the brutal murder except that the peddler had told how he had been "attacked by thugs the night before in the tavern" and that he was worried for fear they would follow him and rob him.

As there wasn't sufficient evidence to do the officials any good—or Micah Rood any harm—the poor old peddler was carried off and buried in Potters Field. But by no means was the case closed.

A few days later when Micah went out to spade his garden, he noticed that the buds on his apple tree were redder than usual, and when that tree blossomed, it was, for the very first time, deep pink instead of snow white. Looking closely at the branches, Micah discovered that every one of the waxy petals was streaked with scarlet, like a trickle of blood on fresh-fallen snow.

Shivers ran up and down his spine, his heart pounded, and felt dizzy as he said to himself, "Could Solomon put a curse on me through that apple tree?" Nonsense! Every apple tree has a few pink blossoms. And then, although there wasn't a trace of a breeze, a whole cloud of petals fell to the ground, and those that stuck to his garments were blood red!

Spring turned into summer, and summer into autumn, and Micah Rood was a frightened man. He lost his appetite, he neglected his fields, he had horrible nightmares. His hair, which up to now had been black, turned steel gray, then white. Neighbors noted the change in Micah Rood and talked about it.

Now, he burned a candle every night, but wherever he peered with his beady eyes, he thought he saw in the shadows, the kindly, wrinkled face of the old man he had murdered, and he wished he had never laid eyes on those sparkling diamonds.

It was a few days before Halloween that year when Micah heard some boys creeping through the uncut grass toward his apple tree. Sensing their purpose, he shouted, "Go ahead, boys! Take all ye can. I don't want the acursed things. They'll do nobody any good."

And there was more truth in that statement than Micah Rood imagined.

In those days, Halloween wasn't celebrated the way it is today. Pumpkins were too precious to be scooped out to serve as children's lanterns, and linen sheets too valuable to be used for ghostly shrouds. Parties were held to be sure, and they were gay gatherings at the more prosperous farm houses, with big outdoor bonfires followed by a midnight supper and dancing and games. The girls pared apples and flung the spiral of peeling over their shoulders to see if it would form the initial of their future husbands. Then the apple was halved, quartered and eaten with a sprinkle of salt to bring out the flavor.

One young lady had just cut her apple when she turned pale and cried, "Look! Look at what's happened to this apple! It's got a drop of blood in it."

Sure enough, close to the core, they all saw what appeared to be a drop of blood, and, will you believe it? every apple which had been picked from Micah Rood's tree had the same sinister stain.

Just then, the boy who had swiped the apples from the tree the year before, remembered he had put one apple in his mother's bureau drawer to ripen, and rushing cross lots to his house, he found it and fetched it back to the Halloween party. It was quickly sliced, and while the inside was dry, woody and rather yellowish, it did not have a single stain of red!

Handed from one man to another, it was finally placed on the mantel, and then they noticed, that the dried-up apple resembled Old Solomon's face!

Everybody began to talk, remembering how they never had been quite satisfied with the explanation of Solomon's death. Finally, the sheriff sent a posse to question Micah again. His door was securely barred and no answer came to their loud and repeated knockings.

When finally the door was forced, there, sitting stiffly in his chair by the window, his glassy gaze upon the gnarled old apple tree, was the miser. He had been dead for some time.

There are folks in Connecticut today who will swear that long after the hermit's cabin had fallen into decay, each spring the tree of Micah Rood had deep red buds, blossoms tinged with scarlet, and each autumn it brought forth its accusing crop of bloodstained apples.

And I am told that scions from that particular tree are still to be found in Franklin County, Connecticut, today.

But I am wondering . . . . what Micah Rood did with the diamonds.

Runaway Locomotives

YOU KNOW THAT many men like to hang around fire stations and chase red wagons. Fewer in number, but just as rabid, are the "railroad fans," who hang around railroad yards and wish that just once they could climb aboard an engine and open up the throttle.

Two such enthusiasts were Tom and Bill, up in Worcester, and one Saturday night in January 1912, when they were outside the South Worcester roundhouse, Tom said, "Wouldn't this be a pretty night to go to New York!"

Bill, gazing fondly at an old switch engine standing nearby with her fire banked, said, "Yeah. It would be a peach of a night."

Strolling over to the locomotive, he patted her warm fat flank and noted that she was coupled to a box car and a "flat" filled with cinders. Casually he climbed into the cab, and Tom followed him. They didn't say much, just looked around a bit, and then Tom stoked the fire, and as the steam gauge started to rise, Bill laid his hand reverently on the throttle. This was a plain case of "two minds with but a single thought," and just to find out how it would feel to start a locomotive, just a LITTLE bit, Bill opened her up. The old engine gave a couple of snorts and a puff, and creaked and groaned, and then, by golly, she started to roll, and before the boys realized what they were doing, the engine and the box car and the flat filled with cinders were out of the yard and onto the main line.

It was a beautiful night to take a train ride, and as the track was clear and all the lights green, Bill opened the throttle, wide! And away they went, over bridges and around curves, and through towns they'd never heard of before. Tom wanted to turn on the headlight, ring the bell and toot the whistle, but Bill said, "Better not. Somebody might see us."

And so, like a ghost train they went rattling along, through Auburn, North Oxford, Oxford Center and Webster; then crossing the state line, they headed for Putnam, Connecticut, with their ultimate destination Little Old New York.

At the Webster depot, Carl White the freight agent was fixing up to go home, when whish! something big and black went by with a bang that shook the whole station. Carl grabbed his telegraph key, called Worcester and inquired, "What went through here just now with no lights?"

The Worcester operator wired back, "Nothing. What have you been drinking? There's nothing on the iron but the boat train due at your place in five minutes."

Poor Mr. White didn't know what to think as off in the distance he heard the boat train's whistle and saw her headlight shining on the track.

When Tom and Bill went through Webster, they set the automatic signal—DANGER—so naturally the engineer of the boat train slowed down and waited. Finding nothing in his way, he lined up the signal and moved on slowly into the city, where the semaphore was against him.

"Hey," he yelled to Carl White. "Give us a green light, will you? There's nothing moving round here."

"Oh, yes there is!" Carl said, shaking. "There's a ghost train with no lights, no bell, no whistle, running all over Massachusetts and Connecticut. Went through here like a bat out of hell. Wait a minute! Listen! He's coming back! BACK UP YOUR TRAIN, or he'll hit you head on!"

They backed, but it was too late.

Tom and Bill had discovered they didn't know the way to New York, so they decided to skedaddle back to Worcester before anyone caught them, and it wasn't until they reached Perryville that they remembered the New London train was due. Down the grade they roared, a sizzling, swaying mass of steel and smoke. When they lurched over the Main Street crossing in Webster, they were doing sixty miles an hour, and only a little less than that when they smashed into the boat train. Folks three miles away heard the crash, and it being Saturday night, a big crowd rushed to the scene, now lighted by the glare of flames as the wreckage caught fire and burned.

Several were injured, but no one was killed, and the joy

riders served their time, which is the reason I have not used their full names.

That's a pretty good story for railroad fans, but best of all is one told me by Carl Warton of the Boston *Sunday Herald.*

Seems that one crisp, October afternoon in 1883, Engineer Mose Smith and his fireman Frank Brown of the engine "Andover" were backing a string of gravel cars onto a side track at Wamesit, just above Lowell, Massachusetts, so the five-fifteen from Boston could go by, when they saw to their horror that the switch at the other end of the siding was wide open.

It was too late to close the switch because the five-fifteen was already puffing up the grade, so Engineer Smith did the only thing he could do. Mind you, he was backing up and pushing the cars ahead of him. And they didn't have air brakes to clamp on, in those days. Smith's only hope was to reverse the "Andover," get her going ahead and get back on the main track out of the way of the oncoming train from Boston.

The "Andover" wheezed and spluttered and shivered and shook as she struggled to grind her way ahead, but the momentum of the gravel cars held her back, and the five-fifteen was coming fast! The men saw there was no way of avoiding a big bump, so Smith yelled, "You jump out your side, Frank; I'll jump from here." And with flying leaps both men cleared the rail and went head over heels down the bank into the cinders.

The engineer of the passenger train applied his brakes of course, but he hit the work train a smart clip. The pins between the cars held, but the most important connection of all, the pin that linked the cars to the locomotive, let go, and once relieved of her burden, the "Andover" did what she'd been trying to do all along; she went hurtling down track, all alone, under a full head of steam!

When Smith and Brown heard that coupling snap, they dashed up the bank hoping to get aboard the "Andover" and throttle her down. But the old gal was too fast for them; she kept gaining and gaining, and finally disappeared round the bend, belching smoke and sparks. She was headed down grade on a clear track, straight for the center of the city of Lowell.

She was soon out of sight, but the men could still hear her barking. Remember how those old engines used to bark when the lever was "down in the corner"? Well, that's the way the "Andover" sounded—a wild, free, fire-belching locomotive on the loose!

A few miles farther on, the track crossed a flimsy wooden trestle that curved like a horse-shoe as it crossed the Concord River, and Engineer Smith said to his fireman, "Frank, one thing is sartin. She'll never make that curve. We'll hear her splash and blow up any minute now."

But the proud "Andover" had other ideas. She was headed for town, and she took that trestle like a greased pig, tearing down hill toward Wigginsville, where, according to custom, old Jim Lawler was tending the crossing.

Jim was a loyal old duffer, and he always raised a rumpus if the engineer didn't whistle, two long and two short, as he approached the crossing. This afternoon Jim was waiting as usual with his red flag, for the five-fifteen, when around the bend burst the "Andover" spitting flame, smoke and cinders like a volcano on roller skates.

She went by Jim so fast the vacuum yanked him off his feet, and was he mad! Shaking both fists at the empty runaway engine, he bellowed, "Why don't ye whistle, ye dem fool? I'll report ye for this!"

And now comes the tragic part of this story.

On the outskirts of Lowell, in a little white cottage, lived a seventy-year-old woman named Mary Nutter. Her house was neat as wax, and she was proud that she owed not a penny, except, well, she did owe the Express Company sixty-five cents or so for delivering a bundle the day before. To owe anyone even a few cents for more than over night was unthinkable; she would hustle right down and pay that bill before the office closed.

At her gate, she paused and looked at the well-kept lawn and garden. It was a nice fall day, and the afternoon sun fell full and strong on waving clusters of purple asters. An hour later, Mrs. Nutter crossed Central Street and walked into the express office.

The terminal for the local trains from Boston was a dead-end track in Lowell station, right in the heart of the city. The station was a long, low brick building with business offices on a side street, the waiting room in front, and the express office in back. Adjacent to all this was the big, open, train shed with its platforms.

Inside the express office, two clerks, Cornelius Paul and Eddie Rand were working on their books when Mrs. Nutter appeared. She laid a dollar bill on the counter, and said, pleasantly, "I want to pay my bill."

Just then, all three heard a strange, rumbling, roaring sound. The clerks knew it couldn't be the five-fifteen from Boston ahead of time, and making all that noise. It was the "Andover," running wild and red hot, and when she burst into the train shed and struck the bumpers, they split like pipestems. Then the runaway locomotive leaped off the rails and ploughed headlong right through the solid brick wall of the Lowell depot.

That runaway locomotive smashed its way the whole length of the express office, crushing desks and filing cabinets, tearing down walls and ripping up the floor. When she came to the farther wall she tore through that in a shower of bricks, into the waiting room, where with a mighty explosion of smoke, steam, dust and falling bricks she broke through the floor and dropped with a terrific crash into the basement.

The whole city of Lowell heard that crash, someone pulled a fire alarm box; firemen came to play hose streams on the burning wreckage, police and railroad officials searched the debris for victims. The two clerks were found dazed, not seriously injured. But poor Mrs. Nutter's dress had caught on the cab, and she was crushed.

The "Andover" lay like a wounded giant, snorting and hissing her defiance in the steaming ruins of the railroad station.

Steamer *Portland*

PART ONE

NO YANKEE BORN and raised on the New England coast in my time is likely to forget the Thanksgiving week-end storm of 1898 when the steamer *Portland* was lost with all on board.

Years afterward, on blustery nights when our little house shook as if it would fly from the foundations, and swirling snow drifted to the top of the pantry windows, my father would drag a rug across the bottom of the door to keep the snow from sifting in, and bank the fire, while Mother put papers around the geraniums. Then she would breathe on the thickly-frosted window pane for one last look out at the raging blizzard and invariably say, " 'Twas just such a night as this that the *Portland* went down!" The way she said it gave me goose-pimples, and I still shudder on wild winter nights when the surf flies high and the wind howls.

One might think that after a lapse of more than fifty years, the story of the sinking of the steamer *Portland* would be old stuff, but such is not the case. The merest mention of it over the radio or in the newspapers brings forth a flood of letters. Following a broadcast which I gave in 1950 dealing with weather conditions on Saturday, November 26, 1898, we received over four hundred letters, post cards, telegrams and phone calls, most of them stating emphatically that (contrary to the records of the United States Weather Bureau) it was snowing at 7 P.M. when the big side wheeler cast off her lines from India wharf and sailed down Boston harbor.

It might also be assumed that after all the details of this shipwreck were printed in the newspapers of 1898 and then re-hashed and published by New England papers on each anniversary, nothing new could be added to this tragic saga of the sea; but to everyone's surprise, several new bits of "evidence" and "never-told-before" stories have come to light. Leaving the so-called "evidence" to others, I broadcast these little-known stories over the radio, and was immediately besieged with requests for copies of the scripts. It was impossible to type out and mail so much material, but I promised that if I ever did put *Yankee Yarns* into book form, I would include these sidelights on the *Portland* disaster.

The first story concerns the experiences of Charles Ward, a modest little man of Chatham, Massachusetts, who worked at various trades off and on but was principally known on Cape Cod as "district man" for the Boston *Herald*. Each week Charles Ward toured the lower Cape on foot or with his horse and buggy, gathering news: births, marriages and deaths, the results of local elections, arrests for petty crimes, and an occasional fire. But as dozens of other correspondents were sending similar stuff to the *Herald*, only the most important items ever got into print.

Ward noticed, however, that whenever he sent in a story of a shipwreck, the *Herald* used it, and as there were many more wrecks on Cape Cod then than now, he was kept busy. To help him get this type of news, he had reliable friends in every village from Sandwich to Provincetown, watching the sea, and at the first sign of a vessel in distress they telephoned Ward, and he was on his way.

Awakening on Sunday morning, November 27, 1898, after a wild night of lashing wind and pounding surf, Ward had breakfast, then bundled up and went out to survey the storm's damage. Broken branches covered his lawn, parts of rooftops and loose shingles littered the streets, and down along the water front every wharf was flooded. Obviously, the coast had taken a terrific beating, and Ward was sure some ships must have foundered.

Trying to make contact with his assistants, he found the telephone dead. All lines were dead; in fact every telephone pole for miles was down, and farther up the Cape, heavy, wet snow had broken the wires. Ward was told that workmen had been sent out to make repairs and that by tomorrow, service would be restored.

Monday morning came, but there were still no phones, so Ward hitched up his horse and drove twenty miles over rutted roads, through mud and snow, till he reached Hyannis. At Chatham, wind and high tides had taken their toll but snow lay only in patches; here in Hyannis drifts were deep, wires and branches in a tangle, and many boats, having broken their moorings, had been dashed to pieces. A large number of schooners had sought shelter in Hyannis harbor, only to be wrecked there. Coastwise steamers were reported lost or in trouble, including the steamer *Portland*, long over due on her regular run from Boston to Portland, Maine.

In a few hours, Charles Ward had three notebooks filled with storm stories, but, before starting for home where he intended to sort out his items for the Boston *Herald*, Ward tried once more to reach his assistants, especially those in Orleans, Wellfleet and Provincetown. No luck; wires still down. But to his great surprise he did get a response from Truro, by telegraph. The private line from Highland Light to Hyannis, over which Observer Isaac M. Small sent daily reports of incoming ships, had been temporarily repaired, and in answer to Ward's query, "How's things at Highland?" the telegraph receiver sputtered furiously.

As the message came in code, the Hyannis operator transcribed on sheets of paper, handing his penciled scribbles to the *Herald* man: Wrst strm in yrs . . . part of cliff gone . . . wind over 100 mph . . . bad wshout btwen Truro and Ptown . . . sevrl schooners on beach . . . wrckage piling up. And then, the operator gave a start and bent closer to the telegraph sounder. Ward saw the operator write the words, "WE THINK STR PORTLAND PILED UP ON PEAKED HILL BARS SUNDAY. BELIEVE ALL PERISHED. 5 BODIES ASHORE. HAVE MUCH

WRECKAGE INCLUDING TONNAGE BOARD MARKED 2283. LOOKS LIKE PORTLAND. NOT SURE." The message stopped, for the line had gone dead again.

Ward, his heart pounding as never before, controlled his emotion, and said, "Let's not discuss this *Portland* angle until we are sure. It could be the *Pentagoet* or *Horatio Hall.* Both steamers were sighted off Highland on Saturday." Scooping up his notes, he went out on the street.

It would have been natural to shout, "The *Portland*'s foundered with all hands! *Portland*'s gone down off Peaked Hill Bars!" but Charles Ward, realizing he had a tremendous scoop, wanted to be sure of his facts before he gave them to his newspaper. Remembering that a Hyannis friend kept a *Ship's Register,* Ward sloshed through the freezing slush to his house, and finding other oldtime captains present, told them in confidence what he had just heard from Highland Light. One man put down his pipe to say, "Yes, I did hear that Capt. Sparrow of the Life Saving Service said he saw two steamers pitching and tossing off Peaked Hill. One was the freighter *Pentagoet,* bound for Rockland, Maine, and the other, being a big side wheeler, looked like the *Portland.* But what in tarnation would she be doing way down here?"

Just then, the skipper pawing through the pages of the *Register,* found what he was looking for. "Here 'tis, right here. Steamer *Portland.* Side wheeler. Built at Bath, Maine, 1890. Length 291 feet. Beam 42. Tonnage 2283!"

That settled it for Charles Ward. Thanking his friends for their help, he warmed his hands at the fire, then put on his coat and hustled to the Hyannis railroad yard, where a work train was making up to do a repair job up the Cape. It was now 6:30 Monday night, and dark as pitch. A second storm was brewing; icy rain, turning to sleet, beat around the railroad men as they piled picks and shovels and loose lumber onto the work train, which, after several attempts to start on the slippery rails, finally got under way.

Ward slumped into a seat in the caboose and dropped off to sleep, but he was brought to his feet with a jerk when the train stopped short, its glaring headlight revealing an expanse of black water into which the tracks disappeared. The train had proceeded only as far as East Sandwich. Water was everywhere, and twisted tree tops and uprooted trunks, parts of broken bridges and buildings, telegraph poles and wires in one great mass completely blocked the right of way. Floating, bottom up, in the middle of this new lake was a small house!

"End of the line!" the conductor called facetiously. "Everybody out!"

As the workmen poked among the debris, their lanterns flickering in the fast falling snow, Charles Ward made his way over mud covered boards and fallen trees, skirting the washout until he found where the tracks emerged from the water and led over a small rise. Stepping gingerly between the rails, he went ahead, feeling his way a step at a time, head down to keep the sleet out of his eyes. Icy water suddenly filled his overshoes and lapped around his ankles; the track was again under water, but Ward kept on, determined to get where he could telephone his momentous news to the Boston *Herald*.

It is hard work walking on railroad ties even in daylight, but in the dead of night, with the ties slippery and under water, Charles Ward found it exceedingly difficult to keep his footing. At one spot, he sensed, rather than saw, that he was on a trestle, but since he couldn't see, he wasn't dizzy and crossed safely. It seemed hours, until far ahead he saw the lights of Sandwich village and left the tracks for the main road.

The going was better now—the road bare where the terrific wind had blown away the snow, but here and there five foot drifts. As daylight came, he noted farm buildings ahead, and, struggling through deep snow, he reached the barn. A farmer, finishing his morning milking, helped him inside and brought him hot coffee from the kitchen.

"No telephones to Boston," the farmer said, "but you can take one of my horses."

Ward, feeling somewhat better, mounted the work horse and continued on, arriving in Buzzards Bay in time to board the first train leaving for Boston since the storm began. Here, too, all talk was of the winter hurricane, the enormous damage done on land and sea, and everyone asking, "What news of the *Portland?*" At Braintree a reporter from the Boston *Journal* sat down beside Ward and told of his experiences—Ward let him talk on, without giving the slightest hint that in his pocket was the biggest of all the stories about the storm.

The train arrived at Boston shortly after 11 A.M. but it took the Chatham correspondent half an hour, slipping and sliding through narrow paths cut in the waist-high drifts, to reach Newspaper Row—Ward was so weak and exhausted he had to stop every few yards and lean against the buildings to get his breath. When he reached the *Herald* office, he had hard work climbing the stairs to the city room.

As he rested on the second floor landing, he heard someone say, "We've just got word that the *Portland* is safe in Provincetown harbor!" Still, he said nothing.

Inside the *Herald* city room was a bedlam of re-write men, reporters, copy boys and weary-faced editors. Dozens of outsiders, anxious for word of some loved one, stood in heavy coats in the overheated, noisy, smoke-filled room. Edging his way through the crowd, Charles Ward tried to reach the editor's desk, but was brushed aside. Bells were ringing, men shouting, typewriters clacking, and suddenly Ward felt ill. The room swam before his eyes and he collapsed onto a desk.

He was carried to a back room, laid on a couch, and someone broke out a bottle of brandy. The editor of the *Herald* bent over him. "Why, it's Mr. Ward from Chatham. You fainted, Charlie . . . all right now?"

Ward nodded, and, reaching for the notes inside his pocket, he whispered, "The *Portland*'s gone . . . struck Peaked Hill Bars . . . everyone perished. It's all here." He closed his eyes, settled back, then, faintly, "I walked and rode all the way to bring this. . . ." and his voice trailed off as he sank into unconsciousness.

Quickly, the editor thumbed through the notes from Highland Light: Great mass of wreckage from str. *Portland*. 5 bodies ashore. Tonnage board marked 2283.

He turned from Ward, grabbed the phone, called the Portland Steam Packet Company office and asked excitedly,

"What's the *Portland*'s tonnage? . . . . Two-two-eight-three? I'm afraid that does it! She went down last Sunday off Highland Light! We're getting out an extra!"

Actually, the whole story was told in the big black headlines spread across the *Herald*'s front page. But clever re-write men, making up a story of what probably happened, lengthened it out, and added opinions of experienced mariners. Hastily painted bulletins were hung in front of the *Herald* office and Newspaper Row was soon packed with hundreds of excited people.

"One man gave me a dollar bill and wouldn't wait for his change!" a newsboy gasped, grabbing his third bundle of extras. "This is something!"

In his hotel room, after a hot buttered rum and a whopping big steak supper, Charles Ward relaxed, a blanket around his shoulders, his nearly frozen feet in a tub of hot water. As he dozed, deeply content, he could hear the newsboys on the street shouting, "Steamer *Portland* lost . . . read all about it!"–HIS STORY!

PART TWO

Another bit of clever newspaper reporting was pulled off by Frank P. Sibley, for forty years a beloved member of the Boston *Globe* family, and its celebrated war correspondent in France with the Yankee Division during World War I.

At the time of the *Portland* disaster, Sib was twenty-six years old–a tall, soft-spoken, gangling guy with a winning smile. He had been a temporary lighthouse keeper, a lumper in a wholesale drug concern, a piano tuner and a medical student, but always in his breast there burned a deep desire to be a newspaper reporter. In 1898, he had a part time job on the Boston *Journal*, covering luncheon speeches, church conventions and minor political shindigs.

Years later, Sibley recalled many details of the devastating storm of '98 as we talked and smoked and shared cocktails in his comfortable apartment in Somerville. It was as simple for him to rattle off incidents about the *Portland* gale as for me to grab a handful of lantern slides and project them on a screen.

"You bet I remember that Saturday," he said. "It was exceptionally mild in the morning but got colder in the afternoon. I had to cover Burton Holmes' lecture on 'Far Off Hawaii' at the Music Hall. Holmes was showing his new 'chronomatographs'—first motion pictures I ever saw on film two inches wide. They were wonderful for those times.

"Well, when I came out of Music Hall, there was a huge circle around the sun, the sky had an ominous yellow cast and there was a real bite to the no'th east wind.

"That night," Sib continued, "Teddy Roosevelt lectured in Huntington Hall on 'The Western Movement of the American People.' As I went in, it had just begun to snow, and when we came out two hours later, and took cabs to the Somerset Club, where the Republicans were tendering Teddy a reception, the wind was blowing a gale, sheets of snow were whipping across the Common, and some of the horse cars were already stalled.

"Funny how things come back after all these years . . . I recall how upset Anna Held was, storm bound at the Hotel Touraine. She had just finished an eight weeks' engagement in 'The French Maid' at the Park Theatre, and she was furious 'cause she couldn't get a train to New York."

Trains were delayed at the North Station, and when young Sibley finally hopped off the local at "Linden on the Saugus Branch" at midnight, he landed in a snowdrift up to his middle—and Sib was six foot three.

The next day was Sib's Sunday to work and although he left Linden at eight in the morning, he didn't reach the *Journal* office till four in the afternoon. Trolley cars on the Linden to Broadway line were buried to their tops in drifts. Not a single steam train was moving, and the only vehicles to be seen were the milk men's horse drawn pungs. The only thing running on schedule was the Chelsea ferry, and from it Sib saw many smashed and sunken boats and schooners driven ashore.

Arriving at the *Journal*, he learned that the Wrentham Savings Bank had been robbed at the height of the Saturday night blizzard, and he went out there. Working with police until after midnight, he had to sleep at the *Journal* office. He was excited and happy to have been on a real news story at last, and in the morning he was given an even more important assignment.

"Sibley," said the *Journal*'s city editor, "the steamer *Portland* sailed last Saturday night for Maine and there's been no word from her. The revenue cutter *Dallas* has gone to the North Shore to see if she might have put into

Gloucester or Portsmouth, and the cutter *Acushnet* has steamed to Provincetown to find out if she was blown across the Bay and couldn't get back.

"There's a possibility," the editor continued gravely, "that the *Portland* went down, and if that proves to be true, there'll be one hell of a scramble for names of those on board. I want you to go down to India Wharf and get as many names as you can. Captain Blanchard usually carried a crew of about forty, and between twenty-five and thirty passengers are supposed to have sailed with him last Saturday night." (Actually there were 176 all told, but no one suspected it then.)

Tremendously elated by this assignment, Sib dashed to India Wharf and found the Portland Steam Packet office jammed with anxious people, all asking about the missing steamer and its passengers. The small office was stuffy with stale tobacco smoke and the smell of rubber boots. Stern-faced men stared blankly at the wind-whipped harbor outside, women wept quietly into their handkerchiefs. Sitting close to the pot-bellied stove, a derby jammed over his eyes, a folded chart on his lap, Capt. Hollis Blanchard's brother waited.

Behind the grill of the ticket booth, a tired, unshaven bookkeeper was trying to answer phone calls and at the same time talk to folks who pressed against the counter. "Sorry, we have no news." Sib pushed his way to the cage and asked for the passenger list; he was astounded to find that the purser had taken it with him on the *Portland*.

"Maybe I can be of some help," he said. "At least I can answer the phone for you."

The clerk smiled gratefully, unlatched the gate and moved over so Sib could sit down. The phone rang, and in his soft drawling voice, Sib asked, "May I have your name and address, please? And who is it you are asking for? Your mother and father? Are you positive they sailed on the *Portland?*"

Over and over he answered the frantic calls, filling his notebook with names of anxious relatives, and their addresses, and names of the *Portland*'s passengers as well. Every few hours the *Journal* sent a boy to pick up Sibley's notes. The names were sorted out and reporters dispatched to get "obits" and photographs. Gradually, they were building up as complete and accurate a list as was possible.

Around midnight, after the phone calls had stopped, Bill Feeney of the *Herald* dropped in and Sib was glad to see him. They asked the cop on the Atlantic Avenue beat to fetch them sandwiches and coffee, then made themselves somewhat comfortable for the night.

At seven o'clock the next morning, C. F. Williams, agent for the Steam Packet company, arrived, and told them, "I understand the cutters didn't find a trace, so I've hired the tug *Dudley Pray* to sail down the Bay and speak every incoming ship. If you boys want a breath of fresh air, you can go along; the tug will leave Commercial Wharf in half an hour."

Sibley, with names of nearly thirty passengers to his credit, jumped at the chance, in spite of the high wind and rough water. Feeney, not too good a sailor, hesitated, then decided to make the trip. The *Dudley Pray* puffed away shortly after 9 A.M. and with a speed of twelve knots stood out of the harbor. It was the roughest day Sib had ever seen around Boston, but he kept his feet and his breakfast, making notes as they passed half-sunken ships aground on every island in Boston harbor.

Nearing the tip of Cape Cod, the Boston reporters observed through binoculars many men working on wreckage at Wood End. Eight good-sized fishing smacks had been swept ashore by the giant seas and were all tangled together. Nearby was a new porgy boat, helpless as they, and farther on a big three-master lying on her side, and awash in the surf was the dismasted hull of the schooner *Grace* of Nova Scotia.

As the tug *Pray* rounded Long Point, the United States cutter *Acushnet* was sighted coming toward them from Provincetown. Captain Coffin approached and through his megaphone asked, "Any news of the steamer *Portland*?"

An officer, leaning from the cutter's pilot house window shouted, "YES! She sank last Sunday on Peaked Hill Bars. Lots of her wreckage ashore but all hands are lost!"

Sib and Feeney fully expected the *Dudley Pray* would put in to Provincetown where they could get a carriage and drive to Truro. Instead, the captain spun the wheel sharply and rang the engine room bell–FULL SPEED AHEAD!

Shouting and protesting, they stormed the pilot house, but Captain Coffin barked, "Mr. Williams sent me out here to get news and bring it back, and that's what I'm going to do!"

"But, Captain, it wouldn't take twenty minutes to set us ashore."

"And break my charter? No, sir!"

A small rowboat was lashed to the deck, and Sib begged to take that; Feeney offered the skipper money, but the bronzed old buzzard would not budge. Slamming the pilot house window to keep out the spray, he growled, "If you two fools want to jump in and swim ashore, I can't stop you, but you'll be committing suicide."

So the two reporters remained virtual prisoners as the tug turned around and headed for Boston. Provincetown was now astern, and a few miles away at Highland Light, the biggest story in years was breaking!

Feeney paced up and down, his usually florid face white with rage. Sibley, appearing more complacent, but even madder inside, chewed on the stem of his unlighted pipe. "My God, Bill, if we could get over there," he said, pointing to the now-distant dunes of Truro, "we might be the first. What a sight that must be . . . wreckage . . . bodies . . . everything. . . ."

Little more was said as the *Dudley Pray* pushed through the tumbling waves on the return trip. After a while, the wind softened and died down, the sea leveled and the sun broke through a mass of clouds. As they passed Minot's Light, with Boston Lightship ahead, two tugs appeared, black clouds of smoke billowing from their stubby stacks, their decks swarming with men.

Sibley guessed immediately what had happened: news of the *Portland*'s fate had reached Boston, and these tugs were taking rival reporters to Cape Cod. They came closer, and Feeney, picking up the binoculars, gasped, "Newspaper fellers. *Post* and *Transcript* . . . and there's John Pember! Every damn reporter in Boston there . . . except us."

Thoroughly sick at their predicament, Sibley gestured toward the frothing water between the tugs. "If we jumped in and hollered, they'd heave us a line."

Feeney spat over the side. "I'd hate to depend on it. Do you realize that we have been royally skunked?" And he thumbed his nose at the pilot house.

Before the *Dudley Pray* had time to tie up at Commercial Wharf, the disgusted reporters leaped ashore and headed for Newspaper Row. Sibley, dragging his feet, felt lower than a snake's belly; Bill Feeney, having had more experience, said philosophically, "We can't get the breaks all the time, Sib, and you'll learn that if you stay in this crazy game. If we'd gotten off that damn tug and reached Truro first, we'd been heroes. Now, we're just bums. But what the hell? We tried."

They parted on Washington Street, each for his office. In front of the *Herald,* hundreds were craning their necks to read the bulletin brought in by Charles Ward a few hours before. The *Herald* had a real scoop, and Bill Feeney felt better.

Sibley slunk into the *Journal* office, unobserved, dreading to face even the elevator boy. Somehow, he had failed miserably on his first big assignment in the news game; but he couldn't figure it out, and that made him mad. Bending low over his desk, he fumbled with papers; he didn't notice when the old building began to shake from the vibrations of the presses in the cellar, as they started to roll with an extra edition. He was startled when a hand fell on his shoulder and a pile of *Journal* extras, still warm and damp from the press, slapped on his desk.

"Take a look, Sib!" His editor's finger was resting on a column of names in heavy black type. "This is what you got over the phone, my boy! No other paper has 'em! A real beat for the *Journal!*"

Then other men crowded around, slapped him on the back, praised him. He wasn't a bum after all; he was a hero!

PART THREE

When it was established on Tuesday, November 29, 1898, that the steamer *Portland* had gone down off Peaked Hill Bars, with all hands, the Boston *Globe* immediately dispatched six of its best men to Cape Cod. The first group sailed on a tug bound for Provincetown, while reporters Michael Hennessy, Frank Stanyan and a sketch artist were ordered to Orleans on the first special train to leave the South Station.

William D. Sullivan, the city editor, gave them specific instructions. "Mike, General Taylor wants an over-all story, but don't make it too tragic. No horror stuff—and that goes for the sketches too." And, turning to Stanyan, "All we want from you is a list of positively identified bodies from the *Portland*, and get that death list in here as fast as God will let you."

The *Globe* men were advised to put on long woolen underwear and take sweaters, knitted stocking hats to pull over their ears, and rubber boots, but time was so short they went as they were, in their ordinary city suits, light overcoats and derbies. This was a mistake.

The trip to Buzzards Bay was uneventful, but beyond that were drifted snow, submerged tracks and an overturned switching engine which they had to help shovel out. At Sandwich, the Old Colony railroad had provided pungs and sleighs to take the newsmen four miles to the other side of the washout where an engine and three cars waited to complete the journey down the Cape. Stanyan left the train at Orleans, going at once to the Shattuck House, a summer hotel opened for this emergency and serving as press headquarters. Making sure a bed was reserved for him in the already overcrowded hotel, he got a bite to eat, then slipped out quietly to hunt up the medical examiner, Dr. Samuel T. Davis, who he was told was in charge of identifying the victims.

He found Dr. Davis at Steele's undertaking parlor, poring over a pile of soaked and bedraggled personal effects salvaged from the surf: cards, letters, pocketbooks, and the sodden contents of suitcases and trunks. Clothing—coats, hats, caps, stockings—was spread out to dry; rings, stick pins, false teeth, spectacles were placed in boxes for future checking. Stanyan noted that most of the watches had stopped at 9:17, 9:20 or 9:25, and wondered if this had been Sunday morning, or night. Each little object cast up by the waves would, they hoped, help identify the bodies lying stark and stiff under canvas in the rear of Steele's store.

Stanyan and Dr. Davis arranged to meet at daybreak to

drive to Nauset Beach together; Stanyan had seen enough for one night.

Back at the Shattuck House all was confusion. Additional newsmen from Rhode Island and New York had arrived, along with a score of red-eyed relatives, all clamoring for something to eat and a place to sleep. Cakes, pies and sandwiches had long since disappeared, but huge kettles of soup steamed on the hotel range along with pots of tea and coffee.

Cots had been set up in the frigid summer dining room and then in corridors, and when no more bedding could be borrowed from nearby private homes, blankets were brought in from the stable, portieres pulled down and rugs and carpets dragged in to keep the reporters from freezing. One wag, laying his watch chain across his overcoat, said, "Even a little bit helps when it's as cold as this." All of them turned in fully dressed except for their boots, and none slept well. It was much too cold for comfort and too noisy for sleep. All night, buckets banged and late arrivals pounded on the back door and wood was brought in for the fires. Stanyan was glad when a bright red sunrise sparkled on the frosty window panes. He slapped some icy water on his face, gulped down doughnuts and coffee and went out in the bracing winter air to meet Dr. Davis in his wagon. Soon they were skirting Town Cove, then rattling down the narrow road to Tonset and Nauset Beach beyond.

Leaving the horses at the Coast Guard station, the two men, dreading the work ahead, slid down the dune to the hard packed beach, where for miles wreckage had been hurled ashore, in some places ten feet high.

In spite of the early hour, whole families were there, and individual beach-combers were pulling and hauling at loose boards, floating furniture, boxes and barrels, anything they could get hold of and cart away.

"Regular mooncussers, they be," an old fellow complained, "but I don't 'spose ye can blame 'em for wanting this smashed stuff for fire wood."

Some wanted only metal to sell for junk, and went around with crowbars, prying off pieces of lead, pipe fittings and iron plates. Others carried baskets, picking up glass, sections of mirrors, china and books. Children, unmindful of the cold, waded to their knees to fish out spools of thread, bolts of cloth and tubs of butter and Maple Leaf lard, stamped "John P. Squires, Boston"; older boys vied with each other to haul in barrels of flour and potatoes. There was something for everyone.

No question at all but what this stuff came from the steamer *Portland*. Her broken red plush furniture and white and gold trimmings proved that, and for positive identification there was her life raft, a broken oar, and the big wheel which Rufus Snow salvaged, all plainly stencilled "Str. *Porland*." Stateroom doors and shutters were salvaged by the score (many of them later whittled into letter openers), and other souvenirs, such as porcelain shields bearing stateroom numbers. And of course, every so often, a more gruesome find, the body of a man or woman rolling in the breakers.

Any reporter could have written a colorful, blood-chilling tale about all this, and Stanyan was tempted, but realized if he did, the *Globe* would not print it. Above everything else, General Charles Taylor was a kind-hearted man, and often had been heard to say, "Why make a man's sorrow any heavier to bear than it already is?"

For two long, disheartening days, Frank Stanyan stumbled along the beach, retrieving with numbed fingers various bits of flotsam which might help to identify victims. Nearly forty bodies had been picked up between Chatham and Highland Light, but only fourteen were positively identified. Stanyan was adding another name to his list when a call came for Dr. Davis to go up the beach where a woman's body had been found enmeshed in a fishing trawl —no possible chance of telling who she was.

As Dr. Davis took leave, he pointed to the leaden sky. "Looks like another storm, Mr. Stanyan. And with the wind coming from this quarter, no more bodies will show up here."

Stanyan put away his notebook, said goodbye to the medical examiner and turned toward Orleans. A five mile trek if he followed the main road, only three miles if he tramped along the shore. The sky was clouded over, the wind whistled in from the south, and then fine spits of snow fell, to be blown in clouds over the hard-packed sand. In a few minutes church steeples of the distant town disappeared in the haze, and it was snowing hard. Sand, too, was being blown in Stanyan's face, tingling at first, then stabbing at his eyes. He turned, and tried to walk backward, but this proved impossible, so he climbed half way up a dune and sat down to catch his breath.

The snow had increased rapidly, and he wondered what would happen if a lone reporter should slip and sprain his ankle, or worse still, break a leg—would anyone find him before the tide turned and came crashing onto that littered shore? This thought drove him to the top of the dune where dead brown grasses bent before the gale. Finding a tiny path, he followed it across a field, stumbled over a stone wall, and walked out to the main road. Soon a team came along and Stanyan hailed the sullen-faced driver, hurrying to get home with a load of laths, mouldings and timbers, before the storm increased. Here, sheltered by trees, it seemed warmer; the thick, wet snow ringed every branch and twig "inch deep with pearl." By the time they reached the Shattuck house, the snow had turned to sleet that froze as it fell.

When he entered the hotel office, the crowd gave a shout. "Hey, Stanyan, where were you when the wires went down? We thought maybe you'd started for Boston on foot!"

"Wires down? You mean I can't file my story tonight?"

It was true, the last sagging wire on the few remaining poles had snapped, and again Cape Cod was cut off from the rest of the world.

"That's right. Everything's down between here and Barnstable. Have a drink; you look like you need one."

"No, thanks. What you fellows going to do?"

"We're going to stay right here where it's warm, and have salt fish dinner. Then a game of poker or black jack. And in the morning the line'll be fixed, and we can all file. Come on, have a drink!"

The warm room, the smell of wet clothes, the tobacco

smoke, made Stanyan dizzy. "I'm going out for a minute," he said.

On the porch he took a long breath, rubbed his hand over his aching head and thought to himself, How can I get those names in to the *Globe?* He stepped out into the swirling storm, above the roar of the wind and the crackling of iced branches over head, he could hear breakers pounding on the beach. Tired though he was, he started down the street, drawn forward by a greenish-white glare of lights shining from a small building. Without knowing why, he walked to it, and stepped on the porch to rest.

As he dug the wet snow out of his eyes and ears, he thought he heard the click of a telegraph key—but that was impossible! The nearest telegraph was at the Western Union office, a mile away. Could this be some amateur telegrapher practising? He pushed open the door, and stood inside. Desks, tables, tiers of glass batteries, wires. . . . A young man looked up from a table.

"Yes?"

"Just came in to get warm. My name's Stanyan. I'm with the Boston *Globe*. I may be crazy, but I thought I heard a telegraph."

"You heard the relay over there in the corner. This is the Cape Cod end of the French Cable Station."

Stanyan gasped. "Cable station? Can I send a message to the Boston *Globe?*"

The young man laughed. "Oh, no, sir. We don't touch Boston at all. This cable runs under the ocean between New York and France."

"And how would they send a message to Boston?"

"Over another cable, through London and Canso, Nova Scotia."

"Tell me," said Stanyan, his mind leaping wildly, "can you send a message to France from this room? And then back over the other cable?"

"I suppose so, there's an emergency cut-in somewhere, but I've never used it."

"And what are the rates?"

The clerk drew forth a card and studied it sharply. "Well, for regular messages, it's 25 cents a word from here to France, and the same from London to Nova Scotia, and about 3 cents a word into Quebec, New York or Boston." Then he added hastily, "Half that for press rates."

Stanyan peeled off his coat and sat down. "Get ready, brother, we're going to scoop the world!"

He was so excited he could barely hold his pencil. "TO THE BOSTON GLOBE BOSTON MASS USA," he spelled out. "ORLEANS MASS DEC 1ST 1898. THE FIRST FIFTEEN BODIES FROM THE STEAMER PORTLAND TO BE POSITIVELY IDENTIFIED ARE AS FOLLOWS . . ." and he wrote down the names.

In a matter of seconds, that message sped from Orleans, on Cape Cod, to St. Pierre and Miquelon, then under the wild, dark Atlantic ocean to Brest, France . . . from Brest to London, and from London via British Postal Service to Ireland, then, roughly, 2500 miles to Canso, Nova Scotia, and down the storm-swept coast of New England into Boston. By the time Stanyan got back to his poker-playing pals, his exclusive story was being set in type for the front page of the morning *Globe*, less than one hundred miles away, in Boston.

* * * *

A few years ago, as part of my lecture "Gentlemen of the Press" I told this story at the Boston City Club, and showed pictures of the steamer *Portland*, the cable station at Orleans and Frank Stanyan. The audience liked it and broke into applause.

After the lecture, a little old man came up and took my hand. "You'll never know what you did for me tonight," he said. "We didn't expect by-lines on our stories back in 1898 and we didn't get them. We just did the best we could. You know, after forty years, it made me feel happy to hear all these men applaud what I did on the *Portland* story. I'm Frank Stanyan."

In these days of world shattering events, brought to us by short wave radio, facsimiles and television, when writers, correspondents and photographers are lauded for their achievements and their names known to every family, it gives me genuine pleasure to tell about these three unsung heroes of the *Portland* disaster—three Gentlemen of the Press!